Business System Analysis for IT Consultants

PowerStart Business Analysis

Trond Frantzen

Cataloguing-in-Publication Data

Copyright © 2015 **Trond Frantzen**.

Business System Analysis for IT Consultants: PowerStart Business Analysis

1. Business and system analysis
2. Business and system requirement analysis
3. Business requirements elicitation
4. Business and system requirement process modeling
5. Business and system analysis methodology
6. Business and system requirement
7. Data and Information modeling

You can reach Trond Frantzen at the e-mail address below:

Trond.Frantzen@PowerstartGroup.com

The Subject Matter

Business System Analysis for IT Consultants

PowerStart Business Analysis

Trond Frantzen

Good Words

"The business requirements sessions were a great success. I am grateful I had the opportunity to participate in many of the discovery sessions, and must tell you it was a pleasure working together to define our requirements. It has created an air of excitement in our office."

● Director, Insured Health Services

"Trond is an exceptional individual who can provide any organization with insights they would otherwise not discover about themselves. He is an expert at dragging business requirements and information out of clients that they did not know they even knew."

● Gord Kargus – Senior Consulting Partner
B-diligent Business Solutions Corporation

"Trond has a magical quality. I have seen his work take very complex disasters and using his approach, create a project that has everyone nodding yes to. We all tend to complicate the heck out of everything and Trond has a knack of getting to what is needed vs wanted. Simplification and segmentation of events is the making of a successful project and a happy CFO."

● John Nesbitt – SVP, Business Development
Pathway Communications

"I am pleased to provide a testimonial – and can certainly attest to the quality of the training.

● Ron Kitchen, Manager Applications Support
Business Systems & Risk Management

"I've experienced this on several projects and I couldn't be more enthusiastic! The approach delivers the requirements the first time, right up front."

● Richard Wybou, Senior Project Manager

"This is refreshingly focused on what the user really needs and wants the system to do. You start with one business event and it grows from there organically as you work with the users to gather requirements. I love the comprehensiveness of the process, and the way you deal with the user by asking very specific questions about the event or objects at hand. This analysis system is very easy to learn and if you follow the steps the output is clear and focused. Great book!

● R. Ray, Amazon Reviewer

About the Author

Trond Frantzen is a senior IT and business consultant, an author and leadership consultant. He founded two international companies: The PowerStart Group and PowerPlus Systems Corporation. He is the author of several best-selling business books, developed a multi-million dollar consulting and training business, and has delivered strategic consulting services to scores of clients; and conducted interactive courses and seminars with over 35,000 people.

 Trond was born in Norway, raised in Toronto's west end, graduated from Concordia University, lives in Calgary – the heart of the New West – and is connected to a very large social network of friends.

As a professional with many years of business development experience, and a finalist in the *Entrepreneur of the Year* Oakville Awards of Business Excellence, Trond has been recognized by many professional associations.

Trond's passion is investing in the success of others – people, organizations and his community.

You can connect with Trond on LinkedIn at
http://www.linkedin.com/in/trondfrantzen

Acknowledgements

There are a whole lot of people who have influenced my thinking about business and systems analysis, particularly about the differences between the two.

'Business analysis' is a study of <u>what</u> the business is supposed to do, while 'system analysis' is a study of the systematic behavior of the business – hopefully, based on what it's supposed to do – with an emphasis on its methods and tools; in other words, <u>how</u> it does things. This has led me to the conclusion that pure <u>business analysis</u> is insufficient (and somewhat different in key areas) for just about any information technology project, while <u>system analysis</u> generally misses the foundation of the work required; therefore the result becomes an almost insurmountable challenge for the analysts and software engineers who usually do the work.

My solution to this challenge – which I simply call "**PowerStart Business Analysis**" – has been developed over several years of research and applying the foundations laid down by many other experts, and experience on real projects. The person who influenced me the most was my friend Bob Proctor (star of *The Secret*), who taught me the clear difference between **what** and **how** many years ago, at the beginning of time when wheels were square. From the technical side, the greatest influence has been the late Matt Flavin (who wrote the brilliant *Fundamental Concepts of Information Modeling*).

Professionally, I have to thank Gordon Kargus, a superb senior consultant who has been a client and a colleague of many years; Dr. Bolanle Abudu who has gone over every word with a fine tooth-comb and helped greatly with construction of the book; and Mark Spencer, an awesome positive critic and the best enterprise technology strategist on this side of the international date line.

While I am forever grateful for what I learned from all of them, the best teachers of all have been my corporate and government clients, and their challenging projects. The real life experience of working in the trenches – dealing with issues and problems and people – has made **PowerStart Business Analysis** the solution it is today, which I offer to my consulting colleagues as an open door to successful projects.

Trond Frantzen
Trond.Frantzen@PowerstartGroup.com

Business System Analysis for IT Consultants

PowerStart Business Analysis

Trond Frantzen

Let's Get Started!

You can tackle this book on your own or with a group of your peers. You can do it on your own schedule, when the time suits you. You can do it at the office, or at home, or in a coffee shop, on the bus or the train – anywhere at all.

I understand that we're all wired a little different and we learn in different way. Accordingly, I've combined text and graphic for you to work with in a way that's best for you. You can also see some videos at **https://goo.gl/tNC0fp**, although these will reference additional material which is not part of this book.

Primary Objective of this Book

To convey clearly the elements of an agile, effective and tested method of analysis that will enable you, as a consultant, to deliver lean business requirements for a client organization, quickly and without pain.

The Focus of the Book

- How to overcome the Blank Page Syndrome. (Yes, everyone suffers from this at the start of a project.)

- How to do modern, rapid business requirements analysis – without pain.

- How to deliver documentation of the business requirements really fast – that is both complete and accurate, and lean.

Other Objectives

By the time you get to the end of this book, you will be able to …

- Identify **Business Events**.

- Identify **Business Objects** and their supporting data.

- Develop the **Business Processes** needed to support your client organization.

- Find the questions to ask subject-matter experts, in a specific context, using the **Business Rules Table**.

- Find business requirements that may be "hiding in the shadows" (i.e., eliminate **errors of omission**).

- Understand how to conduct effective **Discovery Sessions** with your clients and subject-matter experts (SMEs).

- Know how to organize and issue a new kind of lean **Business Requirements Document**.

Chapter 1. The Business Event – The Foundation of any System

Contents

We all live in a serial world. Because of this, we tend to do things in chronological order. This creates a challenge when it comes to analysis of any kind. Gathering information (sometimes a bit fuzzy) and synthesizing it into some kind of knowledge we can deal with is definitely not a sequential process. The fact is, when we assimilate information we are constantly jumping in and out of different "states" of knowledge. We then put the information we gather into one context or another based on the *situations, conditions* and *circumstances* that give the information contextual meaning. Primarily, this is because our work (in the world of analysis) consists of contextual knowledge rather than the serial assembly of things.

Our knowledge repository – our brain – is like a neural network consisting of nodes with access paths that are busy (strong) or not so busy (weak). This neural network becomes our 'organized memory' with keys to join bits and pieces of data to form cohesive information (we hope), and blocks of information from which we can extrapolate contextual knowledge.

In terms of functionality, data storage and desired results, computerized systems are not much different from the human brain. Computerized systems – as is also true for non-automated systems – must store data (i.e., *remember things*) to support various *conditions* and *circumstances* they have to deal with. In the context of business system analysis, these are called **business events**.

1.1 What is a Business Event?

A *business event* is an essential business condition, a state, circumstance, situation or requirement that exists – which the target system must respond to or deal with in order to carry on operations to successfully support its key business objectives, goals, mission, direction and vision. A *business event* transcends time and technology; i.e., it does not reflect **how** something is done; it represents **what** must be done without regard to a particular technology.

To summarize, a *business event* is:

1) a state, condition, circumstance, situation or requirement that exists;

2) essential (critical) to the business; and

3) based on time, a decision, situation or third party need.

To you as a consultant, recognizing a *business event* is fundamental to the work you have to do. So, let's explore the different kinds of *business events* and, ultimately, what we do with them.

1.2 The Four Types of Business Events

Business events come in four flavors:

1) **Situation Business Event** – non-controlled
   "The Customer Buys a Product"
   "The Customer Has Exceeded Their Credit Limit"

2) **External Business Event** – based on third party need
   "The Customer Requests a Higher Credit Limit"

3) **Temporal Business Event** – based on time
   "The Customer's Credit Card Expires"
   "It is Time to Increase the Customer's Credit Limit"

4) **Internal Business Event** – based on a decision
   "The Company Decides to Cancel the Customer's Credit Card"

Note in the examples above that a *business event* **never** starts with a verb. That's because a *business event* is not a process. Let's be clear. A *business event* is a condition, state, situation or circumstance that must be supported by a process. (A process, which we'll discuss later, does start with a verb and can support one or more *business events*.)

When a *business event* is identified we don't need to label it as one of the four kinds of *business events* listed above. We leave it unlabeled because, to a client or anyone else who is reading the documentation, a *business event* is simply a *business event*. It's a business circumstance. We don't need to tell them it's temporal or external or anything else. So, why do we have labels (*situation, external, temporal, internal*) for the four different kinds of *business events* then? Because it gives you, the consultant, an opportunity to process what kind of situation or circumstance – *business event* – we are really dealing with.

For example, what's the difference between "**The Company Decides to Pay a Supplier**" and "**It is Time to Pay a Supplier**"? These are two different *business events* that sound the same, but are actually very different.

The first one (an internal *business event* based on a decision) suggests that there is a decision point, and this decision must be reflected in the subsequent process model. The second one (an internal *business event* based on time) suggests that there is no decision involved, it's just <u>time</u> to pay the supplier – perhaps the goods ordered have been received, and it is therefore time to pay the supplier. Whatever the time criteria, this too must be reflected somehow in the supporting process model.

By assessing the type of *business event*, you, the consultant, are able to think through the ramifications and reflect this in the process model and, ultimately, the business requirements.

The most common type of *business event* used by those who are new to this kind of analysis is the temporal *business event* that starts with "**It is Time to …**".

While this truly is a very common type of *business event*, it is also the most common error, mostly because it is simply so easy – and a lazy way – to identify a *business event* as "**It is Time to … (something)**". For example, I have often seen *business events* such as "**It is Time to Receive a Product Shipment from a Supplier**" when it clearly should be "**Product Shipment Arrives from a Supplier**". The arrival of the shipment from the supplier, while expected, is somewhat out of our control, therefore it is an external *business event*. To state "**It is Time to Receive a Product Shipment from a Supplier**" seems a bit awkward and certainly doesn't have the same meaning as "**Product Shipment Arrives from a Supplier**". On the other hand, a *business event* such as, "**It is Time for a Product Shipment from a Supplier to Arrive**" is something else again. This kind of *business event* is within our control, and we must have a planned response for it.

Carefully thinking through the type of *business event* we're dealing with is therefore helpful in stating it well.

1.3 The Different Diagramming Conventions

Business events that are identified to be part of a project's scope are supported by processes and data. In other words, the *business event* is the identified <u>circumstance</u> or <u>condition</u> that the system has to deal with. How the business system "deals with" a *business event* is described, partially, by a diagram that illustrates the supporting business process and data.

It's interesting to note that three distinct notational standards have developed to illustrate a system's processes and data.

The most commonly used and most popular diagramming convention is *Use Case* notation. Developed by Ivar Jacobson as long ago as 1986 and first published in 1992, (***Object-Oriented Software Engineering: A Use-Case Driven Approach***), *Use Cases* were originally intended to specify software systems, not business systems.

More recently, *Business Use Cases* have been introduced. However, from a business perspective – in my opinion – this hasn't been too successful (although many software engineers claim they like it a whole lot) since most IT professionals are using *Use Cases* to specify business requirements with a lot of "how" (the solution architecture) built in. While *Use Cases* theoretically see the target system as a "black box" (i.e., no implementation details or "how" things are done), the fact is this is rarely the case.

The other issue, in my opinion, is that the use of *Use Cases* simply takes too long and the documentation is not very business-friendly. Jacobson himself appears to agree with this, as he has developed the **Essential Unified Process for Software Development**, which integrates principles from the unified process, agile and process improvement camps.

But, importantly, *Use Cases* and the Unified Process and most other analysis methodologies have been developed to assist with software development, not for business development, enhancement or improvement.

On the other hand, the PowerStart Business Analysis approach has as its singular focus the identification and improvement of business processes, regardless of the technology (or lack thereof) that is applied to turn those processes into a "system". While PowerStart Business Analysis recognizes that most "systems" are supported extensively by software, this element is separated from the actual business requirements discovery, as you will see in this book.

In any event, *Use Case* usage is well documented, with hundreds of books available. The fact remains that *Use Cases* are derived from the foundations that came from data modeling and process modeling, and is clearly defined as such in Jacobson's book, **Object-Oriented Software Engineering: A Use-Case Driven Approach**. That being the case, I'm going to discuss how to use a unique approach to business requirements analysis and process modeling which will enable us to be clearly non-physical in our approach to our work.

Recognizing that most analysts have either a data bias or a process bias (although some of us have a business bias), which of these diagramming conventions would be most helpful to you as an analyst?

It really depends on the kind of project you are working on. If you are working on a **data warehouse** type of project (e.g., statistical or actuarial systems) or **geographical information systems** (GIS), you should probably consider using **Object-Relationship Diagrams** (see Fig. 1.2). These diagrams tell you about the relationship between Objects in the context of individual *business events*.

On the other hand, if you are working on a project that's more **process based** (such as a financial system, distribution or relationship management) then it's probably best to use **Business Process Diagrams** (see Fig. 1.1). This kind of diagram shows the data that's needed to support a specific circumstance (*business event*), as well as where the data comes from and what you do with it (i.e., the data flow).

Fig. 1.1: Business Process Diagram

While **Object-Relationship Diagrams** (Fig. 1.2) are commonly used by database analysts and designers, these diagrams are limited to showing a static view of the data that's needed to support a *business event*, but they do not show the activity of the process that supports the *business event*. The reason for this is

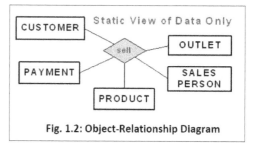

Fig. 1.2: Object-Relationship Diagram

that **Object-Relationship Diagrams** are thought to be data-centric and, therefore, an activity description is not immediately required. However, the set of rules that come from the 'joining' of Objects that participate in a relationship (i.e., the *business event*) – through the 'diamond' in the diagram – are mandatory. These are the business and behavioral rules that define Objects and their relationships, which we will visit later when discussing the **Business Rules Table**.

The **Business Process Diagram** (Fig. 1.1), on the other hand, shows both the activity in the process and the data that's needed to support that activity.

In the end, the diagramming style that you choose should be based on the type of project you are working on. Regardless of the diagramming style you use, everything you need will be there when properly documented (i.e., both diagramming types end up with the necessary information), but the **Object-Relationship Diagram** itself does not visually communicate the process as well as the **Business Process Diagram**. Although it works fine from a data centric view, it's simply not very business-friendly; therefore, while entirely functional, it is contrary to the principles of agile analysis.

1.4 Work-through of a Business Event – Simplified

Before we go on to the details of how to derive the business requirements, let's look at a small, isolated example that's based on a single *business event*.

The *business event*: **A Customer Buys a Product**

The customer enters a shoe store, finds the right shoes (for example, lime green loafers, size 13), and buys them. The customer pays for the shoes. The sales person asks the customer for their phone number and name, and determines if they are already in the store's system. If they are not in the system, the sales person asks the customer for information (such as name, address, phone number, etc.) and enters it in the system. When the customer buys the shoes, and the payment is recorded, the store inventory for 'Lime Green Loafers, Size 13' is reduced by the quantity bought by the customer.

We also need to track the outlet where the customer bought the shoes (so we can have store sales statistics); and we need to know which sales person served the customer (so we can figure out commissions).

That's the scenario. Now, how does the business requirements "specification" for this look? There are two views, one for data warehouse type of projects and another for process-based projects. Each one is described below.

For Data Warehouse Projects

If this was a data warehouse type of system, we would ask the following question to get us started with the diagram:

> What do we need to *know about* or *remember* in order to support the condition (*business event*) "**A Customer Buys a Product**"?

We start by just drawing an unlabelled diamond to represent the joining point – the relationship – that binds the different Objects (or groups of related data) that are needed to support the *business event* "**A Customer Buys a Product**".

Fig. 1.3(a): Object-Relationship Diagram - sell

Clearly, we need to know who the **CUSTOMER** is: We do keep track of customers. So we attach **CUSTOMER** to our diamond.

Fig. 1.3(b): Object-Relationship Diagram - sell

We also have to keep track of the shoes we sell (lime green loafers, size 13) so we can (a) find it in our inventory, and (b) reduce the inventory when we sell some. Let's call this Object **PRODUCT** and join it, too, to our diamond.

Fig. 1.3(c): Object-Relationship Diagram - sell

Because we need to gather statistics to determine store sales, we need to know the store in which the shoes were sold; and (for commission calculations) we need to remember the salesperson who served the customer. We can call these two Objects **OUTLET** and **SALESPERSON**, and attach them to the diamond too.

Fig. 1.3(d): Object-Relationship Diagram - sell

Finally, we need to remember the payment we got from the customer. Let's call it **PAYMENT** (that was easy) and attach it, too, to the diamond.

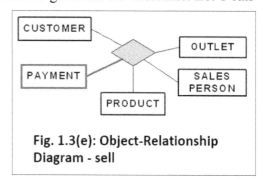

Fig. 1.3(e): Object-Relationship Diagram - sell

That seems to be all the things we need to *know about* or *remember* as part of the process to support the *business event* "**A Customer Buys a Product**". However, we do need to label the diamond, which represents the relationship

Fig. 1.3(f): Object-Relationship Diagram - sell

connecting the Objects – and we have to label it with a single verb. So, what's the relationship? While I'm sure you can think of several possibilities, I'll suggest that the relationship these Objects share is the *selling of shoes*; therefore, I'm going to label the diamond 'sell'.

The reason we join all of these Objects to the diamond is because there are one or more relationships (i.e., business rules) that require the Objects to be connected. Once we have linked (or joined) all the Objects, then we can locate or find the different information (data) that is specific to the *business event* "**A Customer Buys a Product**".

For example, if we know who the **CUSTOMER** is who bought a product in our store (e.g., Buster Brown), we can then find out what kind of **PRODUCT** he bought (lime green loafers, size 13); and the **PAYMENT** he made for that **PRODUCT**; which **SALESPERSON** served the **CUSTOMER**; and in which **OUTLET** (store) he was served.

If, on the other hand, we only know the kind of **PRODUCT** we sold (lime green loafers, size 13), we can then locate or find all the **CUSTOMERs** who bought this

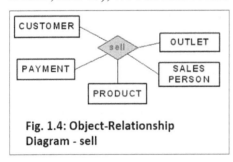

Fig. 1.4: Object-Relationship Diagram - sell

PRODUCT, where they bought it (in which **OUTLET**), who served them (the **SALESPERSON**), and the **PAYMENTs** they made. All of this can be done because these Objects share the relationship of *selling shoes*.

As we develop this Object-Relationship Diagram, we progressively discover the need for each of the Objects. As each one is discovered, we also need to record some information about the Object. For the Object **CUSTOMER**, for example, we know we need to have their name, address and phone number.

CUSTOMER

Someone who requests or buys product or service from the company.

Data Attributes

- customer name
- customer address
- e-mail address
- phone number

Fig. 1.5: Partial Customer Object

Each Object, such as **CUSTOMER**, also needs to have the "business rules" that affect their existence. The table in Fig. 1-6 is populated based on the Objects that participate in a relationship. In this example, we have **SALESPERSON**, **CUSTOMER**, **OUTLET**, **PRODUCT** and **PAYMENT**; all of which are used to populate this particular **Business Rules Table**.

	BRT	Salesperson	Customer	Outlet	Product	Payment
1	Salesperson		N	1,N	N	N
1	Customer	1,N,0		1,N	1,N,0	1,N,0
1	Outlet	N	N		N	N
1	Product	1,N,0	1,N,0	1,N		1,N,0
1	Payment	1,N	1	1	1,N	

Fig. 1.6: Business Rules Table - sell

Specific questions are derived from the **Business Rules Table**, and those questions are directed to the project's subject-matter experts using a specific syntax.

Don't be concerned about how this table is generated. It's very straightforward, and we'll cover it in detail later.

This table, as we work through it, will generate the business rules specifically applicable to the individual Objects. **CUSTOMER** business rules, for example, would look like the example in Fig. 1-7.

Each of the other Objects in the **Business Rules Table** also generates rules applicable to those Objects. Since this is a simplified example, I won't show the descriptions of the other Objects.

After all the Objects have been defined, and data items attributed to each of them, all the rules that describe the relationship between the five Objects will have been completed.

CUSTOMER

Someone who requests or buys product or service from the company.

Business Rules

- may be served by one or more **salesperson**s
- may never be served by a **salesperson** (e.g., the customer never buys anything)
- must have been in one or more **outlet**s
- may buy one or more **product**s
- may never buy a **product** (but must have requested something that was unavailable)
- may make several **payment**s for **product**s purchased
- may never make a **payment** for a **product** (e.g., didn't buy anything, or returned a defective product)

Data Attributes

- customer name
- customer address
- phone number

Fig. 1.7: Object Description - Customer

For Process-based Projects

There is a somewhat different perspective to consider if the project you're working on is a process-based business system, which most systems are. Process diagrams, as distinct from data warehouse type of diagrams, show the data that's needed to support a specific circumstance (*business event*), as well as where the data comes from and what you do with it. Accordingly, we ask the following question to get us started with the diagram:

> 1. How do I know that a "**A Customer Buys a Product**"?

This is followed by two follow-on questions:

> 2. What do I want to do about it?
> 3. What do I need to remember or record?

We start by just drawing an unlabelled circle (a bubble) to represent the process that's going to support the *business event* "**A Customer Buys a Product**".

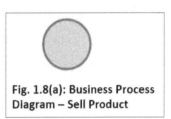

Fig. 1.8(a): Business Process Diagram – Sell Product

The answer to the initial question, *"How do I know that ... a Customer buys a product?"* is that a customer shows up in the store and asks for the lime green loafers, size 13. We can draw this in this manner:

(Just follow along for now. We're going to discuss the details of this process later in the book.)

Fig. 1.8(b): Business Process Diagram – Sell Product

The next question, *"What do I want to do about it?"* requires that you think through all the things you need to do: check if the customer is already in our database; find the lime green loafers, size 13, in inventory and give them to the customer; get a payment for the purchase; record the store in which the transaction took place, and remember which sales person served the customer.

Let's start by determining if the customer is already on file with us, with the following diagram:

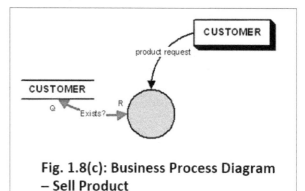

Fig. 1.8(c): Business Process Diagram – Sell Product

If they are not already recorded, get the customer's information and record it.

Fig. 1.8(d): Business Process Diagram – Sell Product

Get the lime green loafers from inventory, and give the shoes and the price to the customer.

Fig. 1.8(e): Business Process Diagram – Sell Product

Decrease the shoe inventory.

Fig. 1.8(f): Business Process Diagram – Sell Product

Receive the payment from the customer, and record it.

Fig. 1.8(g): Business Process Diagram – Sell Product

Record the store where the transaction took place, and the salesperson who served the customer.

Fig. 1.8(h): Business Process Diagram – Sell Product

There's the whole diagram. Now we just need to label it, inside the bubble, with a strong and pointy name to define what this process actually does. Again, I'm going to just label it *sell product*.

Fig. 1.9: Business Process Diagram – Sell Product

A picture might be worth a thousand words, but we can't leave the understanding of this diagram to chance or someone's intuition, so we still have to write the narrative – which could read as follows:

For each request for a product from the customer:
- Find out if the **customer** exists in our system
- Find the **product** sold
- If it is available, give the **product** to the **customer** with the price
- Accept the **payment** from the **customer**
- Remember the **payment**
- Remember the **salesperson** who served the **customer**, and in which **outlet**
- Reduce inventory by the quantity of **product** sold
- If it is a new **customer**, get the customer information from the **customer**.
- Remember the new **customer** information.

There's a specific way of determining the narrative, which we'll discuss in detail later. It certainly isn't some kind of stream of consciousness narrative. How we determine the process narrative is very precise.

As you are going through this process of drawing the diagram and writing the narrative, you also progressively identify the Objects (**CUSTOMER**, **PAYMENT**, **PRODUCT**, **OUTLET**, and **SALESPERSON**), defining and attributing data to them, such as **CUSTOMER** in Fig. 1-10.

CUSTOMER

Someone who requests or buys product or service from the company.

<u>Business Rules</u>

- may be served by one or more **salesperson**s
- may never be served by a **salesperson** (e.g., the customer never buys anything)
- must have been in one or more **outlet**s
- may buy one or more **product**s
- may never buy a **product** (but must have requested something that was unavailable)
- may make several **payment**s for **product**s purchased
- may never make a **payment** for a **product** (e.g., didn't buy anything; or returned a defective product)

<u>Data Attributes</u>

- customer name
- customer address
- phone number

Fig. 1.10: Object Description – Customer

Once this is done you build the **Business Rules Table** by allocating the business rules to the individual Objects.

	BRT	Salesperson	Customer	Outlet	Product	Payment
1	**Salesperson**		N	1,N	N	N
1	**Customer**	1,N,0		1,N	1,N,0	1,N,0
1	**Outlet**	N	N		N	N
1	**Product**	1,N,0	1,N,0	1,N		1,N,0
1	**Payment**	1,N	1	1	1,N	

Fig. 1.11: Business Rules Table – "Sell Product" Business Process

I'll explain everything about the **Business Rules Table** later, in Chapter 3.

In my opinion, **Business Process Diagrams** are much more useful and business-friendly when describing a business process.

Chapter 2. The Business Object – Things to Remember in a Business System

Contents

The first step in business system analysis is not to find out **how** the system will function – the first step is to find *what we need to* **know** in order to support the conditions or circumstances that the business will encounter. In other words, we can't just say, *"what do you want the system to do?"* We first have to determine the circumstances the business has to support, and then we'll figure out how it's going to support those circumstances or conditions.

Figuring out <u>what</u> the business must support is called "analysis". Arriving at a solution as to <u>how</u> the system will do it is called "design" or "architecture". Determining what is needed must always come <u>before</u> determining how to accomplish it – ***"form follows function,"*** as the great architect Louis H. Sullivan wrote.

System design is by definition a solution; and a system solution (*how* the system does what it's supposed to do) is very physical. Business analysis, on the other hand, is obtaining knowledge and therefore not at all physical ... at least, not yet. Analysis uncovers **what we need to know** about a planned approach to a business situation or circumstance, in all its composite pieces; but it is not about how the system will behave. Our analysis, therefore, must be completely free of any implementation bias, or we start trying to mix apples with sheep. What I mean by this is that clarity of thought (without an implementation bias) will always help us get the <u>business requirements</u> done faster and better. And "faster and better" should be the foundation for any "agile" approach to business requirements analysis. The best way I know of maintaining clear and focused thought is to not mix the complexities of a potential design solution with the essential business requirements. How to do this will become clear as we progress.

2.1 How to Base the Business Analysis on an Event

We have traditionally called the result of analysis the *system specification* – because, we presume, it should be specific. The problem, however, is that it has too often been a *generalization* – and much too focused on the *system*; i.e., a statement of the physical environment with general system behavior added. Well, that's been a problem.

To discover the real and complete needs of an organizational unit or a business initiative, all questions and the resulting specification must be put in a specific business context to be understandable. This context, in my opinion, should be a *business event*.

I discussed the idea of a *business event* briefly in section 1.1 What is a Business Event? and section 1.2 The Four Types of Business Events. However, I want to go over this central concept again in more details, since it will be the foundation for all your future projects.

A *business event* is an essential <u>condition</u>, a <u>circumstance</u>, a <u>state</u>, a <u>situation</u> or an <u>external requirement</u> that exists which the business must respond to or deal with in order to carry on operations to successfully meet its key business objectives, goals, mission, direction and vision. A *business event* does not consider technology or specific time; i.e., it does not reflect **how** something is done; it exclusively focuses on **what** must be done without regard to a particular technology or implementation.

In summary, a *business event* is:

1) a state, circumstance, condition, situation or external requirement that exists;
2) essential (critical) to the business; and
3) based on time, a decision, situation or third party need.

All *business events* have a specific structure. To reflect this structure, they come in four different flavors. These are:

<u>Situation Business Event</u> – non-controlled
    "The Customer Buys a Product"
    "The Customer Has Exceeded Their Credit Limit"

<u>External Business Event</u> – based on third party need
    "The Customer Requests a Higher Credit Limit"

<u>Temporal Business Event</u> – based on time
    "The Customer's Credit Card Expires"
    "It is Time to Increase the Customer's Credit Limit"

<u>**Internal Business Event**</u> – based on a decision
   "The Company Decides to Cancel the Customer's Credit Card"

Our first analysis objective on a project is to find just a few *business events* to start with. Although finding as many *business events* as possible is desirable, we don't need to find more than a handful. Once a few have been found, all others will follow. We'll discuss this concept in more detail when we look at the **Business Rules Table** in Chapter 3.

Some other examples of *business events* are:

- A Customer *buys* a Product
- It is Time to *order* a Product from a Supplier
- The Product *arrives* from the Supplier
- An Employment Application *arrives*
- The Company *closes* the Customer's Account

Business event statements consist of nouns and verbs. The nouns usually become Objects (which we'll discuss later), while the verb indicates the context of the process that supports the *business event*.

Note in the examples above that a *business event* <u>never</u> starts with a verb. That's because a *business event* is not a process. It doesn't do anything. A *business event* is a <u>circumstance</u>, <u>condition</u>, <u>state</u> or <u>external requirement</u> that must be supported by a process. But before we try specifying a business process, we need to know what business condition or situation we want to support with that process.

Why the four different flavors of *business events*?

When a *business event* is identified we don't need to label it as this or that kind of *business event* – whether it is Situation, External, Temporal or Internal. Why not? Because, to the organization you are working with and your clients, a *business event* is simply a *business event*. It doesn't need labeling. So why do we have names for the four different kinds of *business events* then? Because it gives you, the analyst, an opportunity to process and think through what kind of *business event* we are really dealing with; and it allows me (in writing this book) to refer to each of the four different kinds of *business events* by a distinct name. But our clients (the business folks and stakeholders) don't care, so it's unnecessary to label them in any documentation that you produce.

But there are distinct differences between the different kinds of *business events* – and that's why I've given them different labels; therefore, it's important to phrase the *business event* correctly.

For example, there's a clear difference between "**The Company Decides to Pay the Supplier**" and "**It is Time to Pay the Supplier**". The first one (an Internal *business event*) suggests that there is a decision point, and this decision point must be reflected in the business specification. The second one (a Temporal *business event*) suggests that there is no decision point, it's just <u>time</u> to pay the supplier – perhaps the time criteria is 30 days after receiving goods from the supplier; or it's "time" to do so immediately after receipt of goods from the supplier. Whatever the time criteria, this too must eventually be reflected in the business specification. By identifying the type of *business event* you are working with, you are then more able to more clearly think through the ramifications on the specification.

Create a short list of potential *business events* for the project

For most projects, it's usually helpful to start with a list of *business events* longer than just a couple. This will give a project a *kick-start* to get it off the ground. To arrive at a potential list of *business events* you need to do some brainstorming, applying a lot of imagination. Your general knowledge about the subject area or target business area will be a great help. One way of brainstorming a project's potential *business events* is to look at your history of *business events* from previous projects. (Yes, you should keep a **Master Business Events List** for your organization.) If you have a Master Business Events List, review each of the *business events* on that list and see how many of them might fit your project. For each *business event* on your master list, change the nouns to fit your project. If you think you have a *business event* that's within the scope of your project include it on your list of potential *business events*.

Don't worry about finding all the *business events* for your project, or even if they are the right ones. Just add the ones you find to your list of potential *business events* for review with your clients and subject-matter experts in an interactive discovery session – they will tell you if a *business event* is within the scope of their planned work or not. Then eliminate those *business events* on your list that your clients or subject-matter experts have determined to be outside the scope of the project and keep the others. Remember that your list of potential *business events* can be quite long or very short in the beginning – but just a few *business events* is enough to start.

After a list of potential *business events* has been created, pick one *business event* to start with and, for that *business event*, ask your clients or subject-matter experts the following question:

"What do we need to <u>know about</u> or <u>remember</u> in order to support this business condition or circumstance?"

When you ask, "*What do we need to **know about**?*" you are looking for input information. When you ask, "*What do we need to **remember**?*" you are looking for what to record or keep track of. This question implies that you are <u>not</u> looking for the process. Your objective is to discover <u>what</u> (data) is needed to support the *business event*, not how things are to be <u>done</u> (the process).

When you ask these questions, your project subject-matter experts will respond with information that could be at the highest level of abstraction (pretty high level stuff) or at the lowest level of detail (right at the desktop level). It is your challenge to decipher what they have said and to determine what an Object is and what's a data attribute. More on how to do that later.

2.2 How to Find the Data You Need

For each *business event* identified as part of the project's scope, we need to identify and illustrate all the data that's required to support the *business event*.

We do this by joining all the required Objects together that we have found to be needed to support the *business event*. The type of diagram in Fig. 2.1 (diamond in the middle, surrounded by boxed Objects) is called an **Object-Relationship Diagram**. It's good for data warehouse type of projects, geographical information systems, or research projects based heavily on repositories of data.

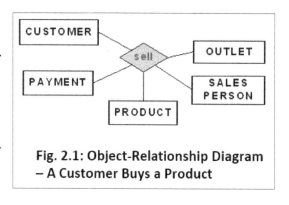

Fig. 2.1: Object-Relationship Diagram – A Customer Buys a Product

The relationship between Objects can also be illustrated as part of a **Business Process Diagram**, like Fig. 2.2 (bubble in the middle, surrounded by Objects between parallel lines). This kind of diagram is usually used when it's desirable to illustrate the business process, such as for marketing or accounting or justice systems.

There isn't much difference between the two types of diagrams, except for conventions established over recent years.

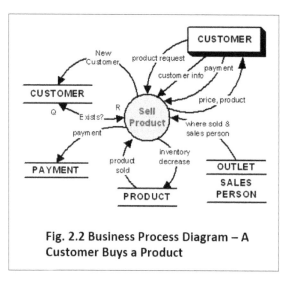

Fig. 2.2 Business Process Diagram – A Customer Buys a Product

There's no rule that says you have to use one or the other of these diagrams – although there are some conventions. But, conventions are often the result of habit, and should sometimes be broken, especially when our knowledge changes. So, use any diagramming method you want. Use the one that you're more comfortable with, and the one that helps you communicate better in your environment. Since there are two schools of thought when it comes to the use of diagrams – data and process – I'm going to use both the **Object-Relationship Diagram** (Fig. 2.1) and the **Business Process Diagram** (Fig. 2.2) to discuss and illustrate each point in this section. Then I'll stop and only go with one of them.

What is an Object?

An Object or *entity* is a noun (i.e., a person, place, thing or concept). It is something that is *essential* or absolutely necessary in order to support the business process or data warehouse that in turn supports the business condition or circumstance (*business event*) found to be in-scope.

An Object contains essential data and information about the business, including rules that govern the behavior of the business under specific circumstances (*business events*). Each Object is a distinct and unique collection of related data about something specific.

An Object must have lots of information to describe it. It must have a <u>description</u>, so everyone can understand what the Object is (and isn't). It must have <u>substance</u> – that is, it must consist of at least two data attributes. Each Object must also include <u>all the rules</u> that govern the business under specific circumstances (i.e., when the Object participates in various business processes with other Objects).

CUSTOMER
Someone who requests or buys product or service from the company.

Business Rules
- must be served by one or more **salesperson**s
- may never be served by **salesperson** (e.g., the customer never buys anything)
- must have been in one or more **outlet**s
- may buy one or more **product**s
- may never buy a **product** (but must have requested something that was unavailable)
- may make several **payment**s for **product**s purchased
- may never make a **payment** for a **product** (e.g., didn't buy anything; or returned a defective product)

Data Attributes
- customer name
- customer address
- phone number

<u>**Unique Identifier**</u>
- customer-ID

Fig. 2.3: Object Description - Customer

Find Objects by asking the Tracking Question

Now that we know what an Object is and what it's composed of, we can go on to the next step in gathering information from a client (or subject-matter expert), as well as how to define the Object and how to draw a picture – we'll use both styles of diagram (Fig. 2.1 and Fig. 2.2) – to illustrate that each Object participates in a 'relationship' with other Objects to support a *business event*.

After a list of potential *business events* is created for the target business system, select just one *business event* (and only ever do one at a time) for which you will develop a requirements specification. For example, you may want to start with the *business event* "**A Customer Buys a Product**". Start by asking a project client or subject matter-expert (SME) the question *"What do we need to <u>know</u>*

__about__ or __remember__ in order to support this business circumstance?" This is the Tracking Question. It must be specific to a *business event*. While your clients will be able to answer the question, perhaps with a little bit of prompting, be aware that they won't rush into answering this question until they are completely comfortable with what you are doing – which takes about a day of interactive 'discovery' sessions.

Also, remember that most systems only do one thing: They keep track of stuff. To keep track of stuff, the system has to record data. One of the main objectives of any business process is to remember what has been done. Remembering what has been done means recording data; and data recorded is data which is kept track of. This, in turn, enables a system to find the things we need to know.

Look and listen for nouns

The way to help your clients or SMEs move along quickly is to look for Objects in obvious places. The best place to start is in the *business event* statement itself. Every *business event* consists of at least a verb and a noun or two. The nouns in the *business event* statement are usually Objects, as long as they consist of two or more data items. Let's look at some examples.

"A Customer Buys a Product".

The noun **CUSTOMER** is an Object – if we can find more than one data item that belongs to it. Well, that doesn't seem too difficult – *name*, *address*, and *phone number*. That's three items (which have to be verified with a SME), so it qualifies as an Object.

CUSTOMER
Data Attributes
• customer name
• customer address
• phone number

The noun **PRODUCT** is also an Object, if we can attribute more than one data item to it. Once again, pretty easy – *product description*, *size*, and *color*. Again, with more than one data item, it qualifies as an Object.

PRODUCT
Data Attributes
• product description
• size
• color

"The Company Decides to Acquire an Asset".

The noun **ASSET** is an Object, if we can attribute more than one data item to it.

ASSET
Data Attributes
• asset description
• asset value
• date acquired

"The Client Opens an Account".

The nouns **CLIENT** and **ACCOUNT** are both Objects, since we can attribute more than one data item to each.

CLIENT
Data Attributes
• client legal name
• client operating name
• client address

ACCOUNT
Data Attributes
• account type
• account number
• minimum amount

"The Company Decides to Issue a Debit Card to a Customer".

The nouns **CUSTOMER** and **DEBIT CARD** are both Objects, since we can attribute more than one data item to each to describe them.

While **DEBIT CARD** is used here as an example, it is just a little bit physical – it represents the design solution to an Object which would be more correctly known as either **PRODUCT** or **ACCOUNT** – but, with the intent of communicating effectively with the client, I would consider it to be sufficiently useful to be included as a business Object.

CUSTOMER
Data Attributes
• customer name
• customer address
• phone number

DEBIT CARD
Data Attributes
• transaction amount
• transaction date
• secret PIN number

What we name something conjures up specific images, and a specific image can turn into a perception (bias) of "a certain way of doing things", or an implementation bias. The word "fax" is a good example. Most of us get a certain image of a fax when we hear the word, usually involving a piece of paper that curls and falls behind the desk; whereas, the unbiased view of the technology would simply be an image or reproduction of the item. For the sake of clear analysis, it's best to stay away from words that create a specific technological image.

"It is Time to Deposit the Customer Payment to a Bank Account".

The nouns **CUSTOMER**, **PAYMENT** and **BANK ACCOUNT** are all Objects, since we can attribute more than one data item to each of them.

By helping the client discover Objects in this way you will find that they will soon get the hang of it and start contributing their own.

CUSTOMER
Data Attributes
• customer name
• customer address
• phone number

PAYMENT
Data Attributes
• payment amount
• payment date
• method of payment

BANK ACCOUNT
Data Attributes
• transaction amount
• transaction date
• transaction type (DR or CR)

For the *business event* "**A Customer Buys a Product**" you will find that you need information about the **PRODUCT** we sold, who we sold it to (the **CUSTOMER**), where we sold it (the **OUTLET**), who served the customer (the **SALESPERSON**), and the **PAYMENT** the customer gave us. All of these Objects can be joined together in either type of diagram. The diamond in Fig. 2.4 is

usually referred to as a "relationship"; and the bubble in Fig. 2.5 is usually called a "process". Both represent the same thing – a situation ("**A Customer Buys a Product**") that needs data and a process to deal with it. Later, in Chapter 4, we'll devote the whole chapter to discussing how to construct a **Business Process Diagram**.

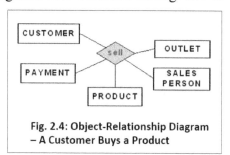

Fig. 2.4: Object-Relationship Diagram – A Customer Buys a Product

Fig. 2.5 Business Process Diagram – A Customer Buys a Product

Listen for nouns with "substance".

In a business model every Object must have two or more data items to have "substance". Anything less than this makes it just another data attribute. So when your client is answering your question – *"What do we need to know about or remember in order to support the business event 'A Customer Buys a Product'?"* – listen very carefully for nouns "with substance". How do you find nouns "with substance"? Ask yourself (*shhh*, quietly, in your inside voice) whether the noun you heard can be decomposed into more than one data element. For example, when we hear the noun **CUSTOMER** can we imagine that we need several data items to describe it? Would we need to know the customer's name, address, phone number, etc? If so – and there are two or more such attributes and characteristics – then we have an Object. If not, then we just have a data item that belongs to some other Object.

It follows that not all nouns are Objects. Some are just data items that belong to and describe Objects. To determine the difference you must ask yourself if the identified noun can be further decomposed – if you can break it down even more. If you can, it's an Object.

Objects are things that we need to <u>know about</u> or <u>remember</u>. To **know about** means we get information from an Object (as some kind of input); and we **remember** things (for future knowledge) by recording items about an Object.

Identify data attributes by listening for nouns that are not Objects.

When a client or SME answers our basic question, *"What do we need to know about or remember in order to support the <u>business event</u> 'A Customer Buys a Product'?"* – and we expand the discussion with them – they will probably tell us all about the many data items that are not Objects. For example, a client may tell us they need to know the *customer name* – you know immediately that this is an item that belongs to the Object **CUSTOMER**, so we attribute it to that Object.

But sometimes we just don't know where a data item belongs. When a client tells us about a series of nouns that are data items and not Objects, but are also clearly related – such as *customer name*, *address*, *phone number* – then we must "roll up" a group of related data items to form a new Object.

It's quite common to find a data item first, before identifying the Object to which it belongs. This means keeping track of stray data items, and when two or more of them seem to belong to an Object that has not yet been identified, that's the time to create and name the new Object and attribute these data items to it.

Ask the <u>Inclusion</u> Question (for Objects).

Often when discussing with a subject-matter expert the process that supports a *business event*, different Objects are mentioned, but it becomes difficult to determine if we really need to include certain Objects to support a specific business process. How can we tell? One way to determine if an Object should be included is to ask the following question:

"If we know about {<u>the OBJECT</u>} what will it <u>enable</u> us to do that we could not do if we didn't know about it?"

Let's look at an example using the *business event* **"It is Time to Deposit the Customer Payment to a Bank Account"**.

First of all, are there any nouns "with substance" in the preceding *business event* statement? Reasonable candidates include the nouns **CUSTOMER**, **PAYMENT** and **BANK ACCOUNT**, since we can imagine more than one data item for each of them.

Our subject-matter expert (SME) for this example tells us that we need to keep track of the **PAYMENT**s that are **DEPOSIT**ed. We also need to know into which **BANK ACCOUNT** the payments are deposited.

As we listen to our SME we are able to identify each of these as proper Objects (they all are nouns, with substance), which we recognized to consist of two or more data attributes, or *things we want to know* about the Objects. But we aren't sure about the Object **DEPOSIT**. The word 'deposit' sounds like a verb, but if we want to *remember* the deposit then it certainly becomes a noun. So, is this really an Object, or is it what we do with the payments? How can we tell? Do we want to remember the payments deposited to the bank account? If so, does the Object **DEPOSIT** have two or more data attributes that don't appear elsewhere? What might these be? What about *date of deposit* and *name of depositor*? Do we want to remember these two items? (Our SME says yes.) Remember that a collection of two or more related data items makes a unique Object.

CUSTOMER
Data Attributes
• customer name
• customer address
• phone number

PAYMENT
Data Attributes
• payment amount
• payment date
• method of payment

BANK ACCOUNT
Data Attributes
• transaction amount
• transaction date
• transaction type (DR or CR)

DEPOSIT
Data Attributes
• date of deposit
• name of depositor
• ~~amount of deposit~~

We also want to remember (record) the *amount of deposit*, but we can determine this by taking the total of the **PAYMENT**s deposited (*payment amount*), so it would be redundant as part of **DEPOSIT**. We can't have redundancy.

What else do we need to know about the **DEPOSIT**? Although it now has two elements of data that we want to remember about it, might there be something else we want to know about it? Clearly, we need to know the **PAYMENT**s that make up the **DEPOSIT** and the **BANK ACCOUNT** the payments are deposited into. We need to remember all of this.

To verify the real need for an Object (such as **DEPOSIT**) we ask the question **"If we know about the DEPOSIT, what will it *enable* us to do that we could not do if we didn't know about it?"** In this example it clearly enables us to know about all the things we stated above – i.e., who deposited what, where and when. By asking our subject-matter expert the *Inclusion Question (for Objects)* it enables us to determine if an Object and its data are really needed to support a process.

Here are two diagrams to illustrate the data that's needed to support the "deposit" process: the **Object-Relationship Diagram** (Fig. 2-6), and the **Business Process Diagram** (Fig. 2-7).

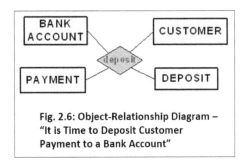

Fig. 2.6: Object-Relationship Diagram – "It is Time to Deposit Customer Payment to a Bank Account"

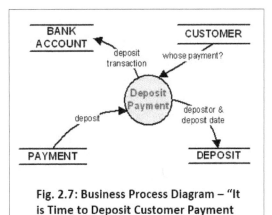

Fig. 2.7: Business Process Diagram – "It is Time to Deposit Customer Payment to a Bank Account"

Ask the <u>Exclusion</u> Question (for Objects).

This is the other side of the mirror of the *Inclusion Question (for Objects)*. It's another way of determining if an Object and its data are needed to support a process.

The *Exclusion Question (for Objects)* determines the consequences of not having available a specific Object, and its data, to support a business process. How can we determine the downside of not having available the information represented by an Object? One way to determine if an Object and its data are needed is to ask the following question:

"If we <u>do not know</u> about {the OBJECT} what will it *prevent* us from doing that we must be able to do?"

Let's look at the same example as before, "**It is Time to Deposit the Customer Payment to a Bank Account**".

As we discussed in the previous example, we know we need to keep track of **PAYMENT**s that are deposited. We also need to know to which **BANK ACCOUNT** they are deposited. We recognize each of these nouns as Objects since they all have two or more data attributes. Just like in our previous example, however, we aren't sure about **DEPOSIT**, even though it does have the legitimate structure of an Object (i.e., it has at least two data attributes).

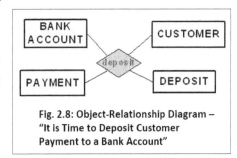

Fig. 2.8: Object-Relationship Diagram – "It is Time to Deposit Customer Payment to a Bank Account"

Also, the **DEPOSIT** Object is "joined" by *foreign keys* to one or more instances of the **PAYMENT** Object – so we can know which specific **PAYMENT**s make up the deposit; and to a single instance of the **BANK ACCOUNT** Object – so we can know where the **PAYMENT** was deposited; and to the **CUSTOMER** Object – so we can know to which customer the deposited payment belongs. But, still, do we really need it, the **DEPOSIT** Object? How can we be sure? To find out let's use the *Exclusion Question (for Objects)*.

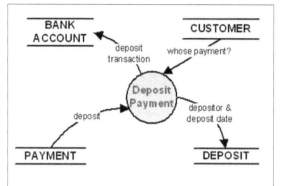

Fig. 2.9: Object-Relationship Diagram – "It is Time to Deposit Customer Payment to a Bank Account"

"If we <u>do not know</u> about the DEPOSIT, what will it *prevent* us from doing that we must be able to do?"

If the **DEPOSIT** Object didn't exist – if the information wasn't available – we wouldn't know about the *date of deposit* and the *name of depositor*. Do we need this? I would suspect so. Without the **DEPOSIT** Object we would still be able to know that certain **PAYMENT**s are associated with specific **BANK ACCOUNT**s and **CUSTOMER**s, but we wouldn't know *by whom* the payments were deposited. Is this key information? If your subject-matter expert says they need to know this, then the Object **DEPOSIT** must be part of the process or data relationship. Therefore, we can't exclude the Object **DEPOSIT** from participating in process that supports the *business event* "**It is Time to Deposit the Customer Payment to a Bank Account**".

On the left are examples of the Objects (with data only) that are needed to support the relationship "deposit" (shown in the **Object-Relationship Diagram**, Fig. 2.8), or the process "Deposit Payment" (shown in the **Business Process Diagram**, Fig. 2.9).

CUSTOMER

<u>Data Attributes</u>

- customer name
- customer address
- phone number

PAYMENT

<u>Data Attributes</u>

- payment amount
- payment date
- method of payment

BANK ACCOUNT

<u>Data Attributes</u>

- transaction amount
- transaction date
- transaction type (DR or CR)

DEPOSIT

<u>Data Attributes</u>

- date of deposit
- name of depositor
- ~~amount of deposit~~

The Symbiotic Relationship between Objects and Processes.

A "process" is inseparable from a "data relationship" – they have a genuine symbiotic relationship. In other words, each *business event* (i.e., circumstance or condition) that needs to be supported by the target business area must be <u>dealt with by that target business area in some manner</u> (a specific process). This always requires <u>the use of data</u> (Objects) – either to retrieve some data or to record some data. It's impossible to have a process that doesn't involve retrieving, viewing or recording of data. It's equally redundant to have data that isn't ever involved in some kind of process – something has to happen to it, otherwise why do we bother recording it? Given this to be true, then it only makes sense to use just one diagram type – the **Business Process Diagram** – to illustrate process and its required data.

When we include an Object in any kind of diagram that supports a *business event*, it represents <u>all the instances</u> of that Object – its history. What distinguishes one occurrence of an Object from another may simply be a *date*.

In the **Business Process Diagram** in Fig. 2.10, for example, the Object **<u>PAYMENT</u>** can be seen as one or more instances of **<u>PAYMENT</u>**s; we can therefore see it as a <u>list</u> of all the payments (i.e., all its occurrences). Equally, the **<u>CUSTOMER</u>** and **<u>PRODUCT</u>** Objects can be seen as <u>lists</u> of all the customers that we have done business with and all the products that we have sold to those customers.

Objects are always named and documented in the singular since we always view them as *one or more instances* of an Object and, as we will learn later when we discuss the **Business Rules Table** in Chapter 3, we always ask questions about an Object as if there was only a single instance of that Object.

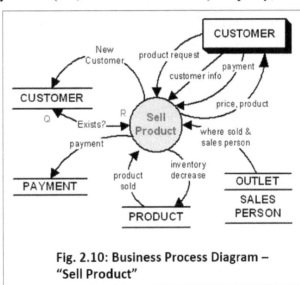

Fig. 2.10: Business Process Diagram – "Sell Product"

Summary of How to Find Business Events and Objects

1. **Create a short list of potential *business events* for the project.** Don't worry about finding all the *business events* that are in-scope – just start with a few. You only need a few *business events* to find all the others, as you will see when we discuss the **Business Rules Table** in Chapter 3.

After an initial list of potential *business events* has been created, pick one *business event* to start with and ask the project subject-matter experts (the ones who have knowledge in the context of the chosen *business event*) the following question:

"What do we need to <u>know about</u> or <u>remember</u> in order to support this business condition or circumstance?"

The purpose of this question is to discover what data is needed to support the *business event*. To then find the data, you need to do the following:

2. **Look and listen for nouns.** Start by looking in the *business event* statement itself. It will consist of at least a verb and a noun or more. The nouns in the *business event* statement are usually Objects, as long as they consist of two or more data items.

3. **Listen for nouns with "substance".** An Object in a business data model must consist of at least two data items. Less is just a data attribute. For example, would the noun **CUSTOMER** need several data items to describe it? Would we need to know the *customer's name*, *address*, *phone number*, etc? If so – and if there are at least two such attributes and characteristics – then we have an Object. If not, then we just have an attribute that belongs to some other Object.

    It follows that all nouns are not Objects. Some are just data attributes that belong to and describe Objects. Others are full Objects. To know the difference you must determine if the piece of data, the noun, can be further decomposed. If you can't further decompose it, it's a data attribute. If you can, it's an Object.

4. **Identify data attributes by listening for nouns that are not Objects.** Sometimes we just don't know where a data item belongs, mainly because we haven't yet attributed enough data to create a suitable target Object. When a client mentions a series of nouns that are clearly data items and not Objects, but are also undoubtedly related – such as *customer name*, *address*, *phone number* – then we "roll up" a group of related data items to form a new Object that hasn't yet been formed.

???
Data Attributes
• customer name
• customer address
• phone number

5. **Ask the Inclusion Question (for Objects).** For every Object that participates in a *business event* ask the following question:

    "If I know about {<u>the OBJECT</u>} what will it <u>enable</u> us to do that we could not do if we didn't know about it?"

6. **Ask the Exclusion Question (for Objects).** For every Object in a *business event* ask the following question:

> **"If we <u>do not know</u> about {<u>the OBJECT</u>} what will it <u>prevent</u> us from doing that we must be able to do?"**

It's also important to recognize that, so far, we have dealt with the issue of populating an Object with data (data attribution) only at the intuitive level. We have not yet dealt at all with the principles of normalization and data attribution; i.e., how to find the right home (in an Object) for data items, and how do we do so without redundancy? So, we'll look at that now, with an eye to ease of understanding and simplicity.

2.3 What is Normalization Anyway, and why do I Care?

During business system analysis, information that is relevant to the project must be identified, organized and documented. This process of data discovery, data allocation and organization is called *data normalization*. Contrary to popular opinion, this must be done to ensure complete and accurate business requirements. But, also contrary to popular opinion, this doesn't have to take forever in the context of business requirements analysis. Nor does it have to be a technical exercise.

Normalization – what is it?

The purpose of normalization is to structure data in such a way as to eliminate all forms of redundancy and, ultimately, to allow the processing of the data – in a database structure – without inconsistencies or errors. This means that we have to make sure that any single data item (*customer name*, for example) is maintained in one place only, while being available everywhere it is needed.

Normalization, in its conventional packaging, is presented as being a progression of successively improved stages of data purity:

1. **First Normal Form (1NF)** – removes multi-valued data attributes and repeated groups from Objects.

2. **Second Normal Form (2NF)** – removes data attributes from Objects that are dependent on some of the other data attributes.

3. **Third Normal Form (3NF)** – removes data attributes from Objects that are not directly dependent on the Object.

4. **Fourth Normal Form (4NF)** – removes multi-valued dependencies within Objects.

5. **Fifth Normal Form (5NF)** – removes other remaining anomalies.

This is all very interesting, but what does *data normalization* have to do with business system requirements analysis, as I have suggested? And why would we care?

Many technical specialists would argue that you shouldn't care; that worrying about data and its *normalization* is the job of database designers. They would argue that you, as a consultant doing business system analyst, don't need to know a thing about database design (and they are right); nor do you need to know anything about data modeling (again, in the technical sense, they're right). They will tell you that all the technical aspects of data belong in the domain of the database experts. And, of course, they are right.

So, why do you care?

When data is properly attributed to their Objects, and redundancies eliminated, you will then be able to ask highly focused, non-abstract questions of your clients and subject-matter experts. All the questions that you need to ask about their business requirements come <u>from the data</u> (after all, it is data that gives them the information they need from their systems). If the data is just a collection of 'stuff', then it is very difficult to ask meaningful questions. On the other hand, if the data is well organized and non-redundant, you will be able to ask the SMEs very specific and in-context questions about their business requirements, based on the data they need. To be able to find the data, you have to know how to identify it and attribute it properly to Objects. That's *data attribution*. You also have to eliminate the redundancies and data that are hiding behind aliases. That's *data normalization*.

When you allocate data items to Objects, and those Objects are partitioned well, you will achieve the level of detail necessary for good, precise questions for your SMEs, rather than vaguer questions that come from general knowledge. That old saying, *"the devil's in the details"* can be put to rest because proper <u>data attribution</u> and <u>data normalization</u> take the devilish complexity out of finding the questions to ask your clients and SMEs.

A full study of *data normalization* could be an academic endeavor that makes all your other studies pale by comparison. It is not for the weak-of-heart. Tomes have been written about this subject, mostly incomprehensible. Nor would such a study be all that productive. As a practicing consultant who does business analysis, you need <u>to be able to do it</u>, but you don't necessarily need to explain to everyone what it is and how it works in all its theoretical finery. Accordingly, I have prescribed a set of five simple rules that – if you follow all of them all the time – will enable you to achieve sufficiently normalized data attribution and well-partitioned Objects, as part of your business requirements analysis, no less. What this means to you is (a) really good attribution of data to Objects; (b) no redundancy; and, (c) Objects that are ready for inclusion in the **Business Rules**

<u>Table</u> so you can find and ask the detailed questions you have to ask your SMEs. We will explore the Business Rules Table in the next chapter.

2.4 The 5 Rules of Business Data

No redundancy whatsoever is the key to success with data. Follow these rules and you will never look back.

Business Data Rule # 1

- **Attribute the data item to the Object it describes best, and to no other Object.**

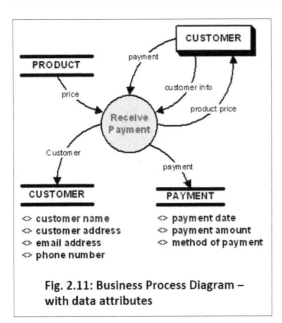

Fig. 2.11: Business Process Diagram – with data attributes

When we speak with our clients and subject-matter experts to determine their business requirements, we hear all kinds of nouns to describe the business. Some of these nouns are Objects. These Objects, in turn, consist of *other nouns* to describe their content.

Those other nouns that describe an Object's content are data items that must be properly attributed to the right Objects. We call this *finding a home for the data* – or attributing data to an Object. But we don't attribute data items to just any old Object. Each data item must be attributed to the Object *it best describes*. And, of course, each data item can only be attributed to one Object.

But sometimes we hear 'stuff' from our clients, and we just don't know where a data item belongs – most likely because we haven't yet set up a named Object to which we can attribute the data we hear. The solution to this situation is to collect seemingly stray data items until we reach critical mass – until a pattern develops. When we have enough data items that are clearly related – such as *customer name*, *address* and *phone number* – then we "roll up" a group of related data items to form a new Object. This is not usually a big challenge since it only takes two data items to make a distinct Object.

CUSTOMER
Data Attributes
- customer name
- customer address
- phone number

???
Data Attributes
- customer name
- customer address
- phone number

Object: An Object or *entity* is a person, place or thing that a business area or target system needs to know about or remember something about.

While an Object is always a noun, it is distinct from other nouns that are simple data attributes because a business Object:

(1) consists of at least two data attributes, to give it substance;

(2) is essential to the successful operation of the target business area or system (i.e., the Object and its data must be present or the business processes will not be able to do what they are supposed to do); and

(3) is defined by specific **business rules** in specific circumstances.

CUSTOMER

Someone who requests or buys product from the company.

Business Rules
- may purchase several **products**
- may never buy a **product** (but must have requested something that was unavailable)
- may make several **payments** for **products** purchased
- may never make a **payment** for a **product** (e.g., didn't buy anything; returned a defective product)

Data Attributes
customer name
customer address
phone number

Fig. 2.12: Customer Object

While it's true that all business Objects must consist of at least two data items to be considered an Object, these Objects can be 'decomposed' to just a single data attribute when designing the database. However, such decomposition comes much later and is not part of business analysis.

Data Attribute: A data attribute is an element of data that is a property of the Object to which it is assigned. A data attribute is defined by a name and description, and eventually represented by a set of values, which may include image and sound. In addition to the business rules that come from the **Business Rules Table** (which we will review in the next Chapter) data attributes are required to define what must be remembered or known about each Object. Fig. 2-12 is an abbreviated example of an Object description (**CUSTOMER**), with governing business rules and data attributes.

Totals and Flags: Totals and 'flags' should not be attributed to Objects, even though it may seem attractive at the time. Neither totals nor 'flags' are real data items; they are the convenient representation of something else. A total can be summed from other data items; therefore it is redundant. A 'flag' is really a status of some kind, which can usually be determined from some other data attribute such as *time* or *amount*, particularly when the *absence* of data will usually represent a specific status. Flags and totals are therefore redundant and are signs of an early design bias, or a pre-design way of keeping track of something. Flags and totals are usually used to improve database access efficiency. It is best to wait until database design is done to "denormalize" with flags and totals, when all the facts about volumes, data throughput and access requirements have been considered. However … on real-life projects, clients and SMEs often tell me they need this and that 'total' to keep track of accumulations.

As a consultant and an analyst, it's counterproductive to start telling them why we shouldn't do this. Accordingly, I often do record their need for these totals (you need to be seen to be communicating effectively, after all), but I make sure the software engineering team understands they aren't really there, so they can design the appropriate way of determining totals.

Business Data Rule # 2

- **Each Object must have a unique identifier. The unique identifier must not be used as "data".**

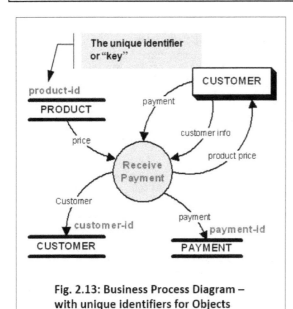

Fig. 2.13: Business Process Diagram – with unique identifiers for Objects

Unique Identifier: A unique identifier is an ID that is unique to a specific instance or occurrence of an Object. An Object's 'unique identifier' is also used as a pointer or link to other Objects that participate in a business process to support a *business event*.

An Object's 'unique identifier' is not to be used as data; that's a design choice (a 'how to'), and not a very good one, in my opinion. It is simply a 'unique identifier' or key.

So, why is it important when dealing with business Objects to discuss *unique identifiers* and *keys*? Well, it's so we can all have the same understanding of how Objects are "joined" to support a business process, in such a way that there is no duplication of data. (**Business Data Rule # 1** eliminates redundancy; therefore data items only appear in one place.)

The data items that are needed to fulfill a business process often belong to different Objects. For example, data like *product description* belongs to the Object **PRODUCT**, while data such as *customer name* belongs to the Object **CUSTOMER**.

If a business process needs to be supported by several different Objects,

Fig. 2.14: Business Process Diagram – "Sell Product"

then all the Objects that are needed must be shown as part of the **Business Process Diagram**.

Additionally, each Object must be non-redundant with respect to data. In other words, a specific data item can appear in one and only one Object, and only once, regardless of the name it uses. This means that a specific Object can only contain information about the subject of that Object, and about no other Object. (See **Business Data Rule #1**.)

This, in turn, means that to get information about one or more of the **PAYMENT**s received from a specific **CUSTOMER**, we need to know who the specific **CUSTOMER** is; and the **CUSTOMER** record (Object) must have a pointer or link of some kind that *joins* it to all the **PAYMENT**s we've received from that **CUSTOMER**. (Each **PAYMENT** is distinguished from the other **PAYMENT**s either by the *date of the payment* or by some other data attribute.) Equally true, then, is that if we know the ID of a specific **PAYMENT**, we will be able to find the **CUSTOMER** to whom it belongs.

So when an Object is shown as being part of a business process, it means that all other Objects (and their data) with which it shares the process can be individually *joined*, based on a pointer or key that connects one Object with another. For example, in Fig. 2.15, if we know who the **CUSTOMER** is, we can find all the **PAYMENT**s they made; and, if we know the **PRODUCT**, we can find all the **CUSTOMER**s who have bought this **PRODUCT**. Since a unique identifier joins each Object with the right data, we don't have to duplicate information in any Object.

CUSTOMER
Someone who requests or buys product from the company.

Business Rules
- may purchase several **products**
- may never buy a **product** (but must have requested something that was unavailable)
- may make several **payments** for **products** purchased
- may never make a **payment** for a **product** (e.g., didn't buy anything; returned a defective product)

Data Attributes
- customer name
- customer address
- phone number

Unique Identifier
- Customer-ID

Pointers to Related Objects
- Salesperson-ID (mv)
- Outlet-ID (mv)
- Product-ID (mv)
- Payment-ID (mv)

Fig. 2.15: Object Description

Pointers to Related Objects: A 'Pointer to a Related Object' is an Object's unique identifier contained within another Object. It is often called a "foreign key", meaning it is the key (unique identifier) of an external Object. The "foreign key" provides the ability to find data from other Objects to support the information needs of a specified business process.

The "joining" of Objects in this manner eliminates the need for data repetition or redundancy. "Foreign keys" can be single-valued (i.e., point to just one occurrence of another Object); or they can be multi-valued (i.e., point to several instances of another Object, using the qualifier "**mv**", which means multi-valued or a variable number of instances of the referenced Object). This ratio of occurrences between Objects is determined from the **Business Rules Table**, which in turn specifies the foreign keys needed for the Conceptual Data Model, which is the prescription for database design. While developing the Conceptual

Data Model is not part of business system analysis, the rules required to enable that design come from front-end business analysis.

It is implicit in each **Business Process Diagram** – such as the one in Fig. 2.16 – that a "relationship" exists between each of the participating Objects. To find the related Objects and data, then, requires that each Object will have a unique identifier and that their respective unique identifiers connect all related Objects.

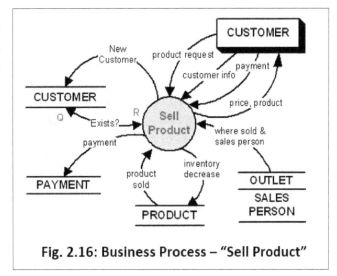

Fig. 2.16: Business Process – "Sell Product"

Business Data Rule # 3

- **Each Object must have two or more data attributes, other than the unique identifier.**

  (Data items can be part of an Object's data set; and can come from the process that supports the relationship.)

All business Objects must consist of at least two data items for the Object to have substance and therefore exist. If an Object does not have two or more data attributes there will be no way to distinguish an Object – *representing a collection of related data about something specific* – from any other noun that happens to be a single data item. This is the business view. From a database modeling perspective, an Object can be *normalized* to a single data item. But that is not the business view.

We sometimes have Objects that appear to be full of redundancy. Let's look at a typical **PURCHASE ORDER** Object as an example. Theoretically, the purchase order should, in addition to the data that's specified in Fig. 2.18 under <u>Data Attributes</u>, also include information such as *product description*, *product cost*, and *supplier name* and *address*.

Of course, the **PURCHASE ORDER** Object doesn't have any of this because all of this data is already found in other Objects. In accordance with our **Business Data**

Rule # 1, *product description* and *product cost* have already been attributed to the Object **PRODUCT**, and *supplier name* and *address* find their home in **SUPPLIER**. If we attributed this data again to **PURCHASE ORDER** then we would be in violation of **Business Data Rule # 1**; that is, we would have attributed data to more than one Object. And we can't do that.

We can't do that because we already have access to this data by way of *foreign keys* or *pointers to related Objects*. You'll remember that each Object must have a unique identifier (**Business Data Rule # 2**). The identifier for **PURCHASE ORDER** in the diagram above is *purchase order-id*. You will also recall that a *foreign key* is one Object's unique

Fig. 2.17: Business Process Diagram – Object Relationships

identifier contained within another Object, as a link. This means that if **PURCHASE ORDER** needs some information that is part of **SUPPLIER**, then **PURCHASE ORDER** will have the unique identifier of **SUPPLIER** as a *foreign key* or link. The same **PURCHASE ORDER** Object (Fig. 2.18) shows the *Pointers to Related Objects* (foreign keys) it needs to have access to data in the Objects **SUPPLIER** (supplier-id), **PRODUCT** (product-id), and **OUTLET** (outlet-id). Also notice that the **PURCHASE ORDER** may refer to several **OUTLET** records, and it does this by using the convention "mv", meaning multi-valued.

PURCHASE ORDER

An agreement to purchase product from an accredited supplier, with specific payment and delivery terms prearranged.

Business Rules
- is issued to one **supplier** only
- may be for one or many **products**
- may be based on many customer **orders**

Unique Identifier
- purchase order-ID

Data Attributes
- quantity ordered
- payment terms (mv)
- currency type
- expected delivery date
- ...
- ...
- ...

Pointers to Related Objects
- supplier-ID
- product-ID
- outlet-ID (mv)

Fig. 2.18: Object description – Foreign Keys and Data

Data often arises from the process that supports a relationship – and that data must be attributed to an Object.

So, what does this mean?

An Object can have data attributed to it that's discovered as part of a supporting process; or, if you like, the data can *arise* out of the process that supports the *business event*. An Object that gets some of its data in this way cannot exist without being dependent on one or more of the other Objects that participate in the relationship. In other words, as shown in Fig. 2.17, if the **SUPPLIER** Object didn't exist in that process then **PURCHASE ORDER** could not exist either. Why not? Because **PURCHASE ORDER** is dependent on the existence of a **SUPPLIER** record to be able to know the *supplier name* and *address*. Equally, if the **PRODUCT** Object went away so would **PURCHASE ORDER** disappear.

The **PURCHASE ORDER** also needs to know what *product* and its *cost* that make up the PO. This means that the **PURCHASE ORDER** is dependent on a specific record (occurrence) of the **PRODUCT** Object.

In the example (Fig. 2.19), the supporting process generates data such as *quantity ordered*, *payment terms*, *currency type* and *expected delivery date*. None of these data items, required by the **PURCHASE ORDER**, could be found in any other Objects, so they were generated by the supporting business process; which could have been done by a person on the phone, or by some kind of automated process, or a combination of both. How it's done is a solution design issue (we don't have to figure it out now). However, what is needed (the data attributes) is an essential business requirement, which must be determined now.

Fig. 2.19: Business Process Diagram – Order Product – Illustrating use of Foreign Keys

An Object that is dependent on other Objects and gets attributed with data in this way is called an *Associative Object*. Most Objects that sound somewhat physical are Associative Objects (such as **PURCHASE ORDER**, **CONTRACT**, **POLICY**, **LICENSE**, **PERMIT**). It's really not important what it's called (since we never label the type of Object in the documentation anyway) but it is important to know how it got its data. All required data that cannot be found in other Objects that participate in the same process (using *foreign keys*) must *arise from the process* that is being defined, and be attributed to the Associative Object.

Business Data Rule # 4

- Any data item that is common to all subtypes of an Object must be attributed to that Object's supertype.

- Any data item that is attributed to one subtype Object cannot be attributed to any other subtype Object (See Business Data Rule # 1).

There are times when we need to refer to something globally, and other times when we need to refer to a distinct part of something. For example, an organization with three different kinds of employees (full-time, part-time and contract employees) may refer to all of their employees (i.e., all three different kinds) under one circumstance, or just to one kind of employee (e.g., full-time) under another circumstance. The individual types of employees – **FULL-TIME EMPLOYEE**, **PART-TIME EMPLOYEE** and **CONTRACT EMPLOYEE** – will each have data that is unique only to them. This type of Object is called a *Subtype Object*. The general reference to an "**EMPLOYEE**" will have data that is common to the three different kinds of employees. This type of Object is called a *Supertype Object*.

Subtypes (such as **FULL-TIME EMPLOYEE**) depend on their supertype for existence because each supertype contains data that is common to all of its subtypes, and is necessary to completely describe those subtypes. Subtypes, however, can be dealt with independently of their supertype. It is usually more precise (and productive) to ask questions of clients and subject-matter experts about the subtype than about the more abstract supertype. For example, when we ask a question about the supertype Object **EMPLOYEE**, we're implying that we include all the different kinds of employees in our questions. On the other hand, when we ask about the subtype Object **FULL-TIME EMPLOYEE**, it's a very specific question that excludes **PART-TIME EMPLOYEE**s and **CONTRACT EMPLOYEE**s. Questions at the subtype level lead to more specific answers than questions at the supertype Object level.

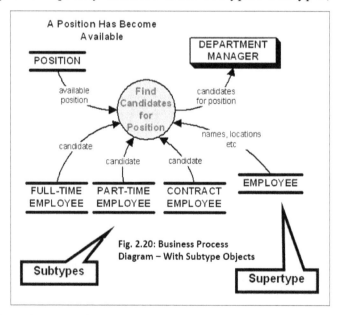

Fig. 2.20: Business Process Diagram – With Subtype Objects

A subtype Object can also be a supertype to its own subtype.

Creating subtype Objects has a singular business objective: It permits you to ask your clients better, more focused and specific questions.

Business Data Rule # 5

- **When a repeating group of related data** (multi-valued data items) **is found in a previously defined Object, create a new Object from the multi-valued data items found.**

Sometimes we bury information inside an Object without realizing it. Using the example in Fig. 2.23 *Moving Rule#5 Data to Create a New Object*, found on the next page, we will see how **Business Data Rule # 5** helps us find Objects within Objects. This, in turn, enables us to ask better questions of our clients, which we will see when we review the **Business Rules Table**. Let's look at an example of discovering "characteristic" Objects using the Object **CUSTOMER** (Fig. 2.22).

To apply Business Data Rule # 5 we first determine if there are any data attributes in the Object that are multi-valued (mv), and seem to be part of a common

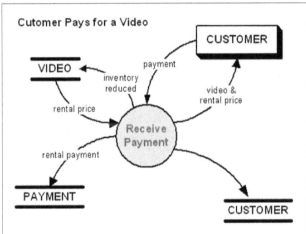

Fig. 2.21: Business Process Diagram – "Receive Payment"

CUSTOMER

Someone who requests or buys product from the company.

Governing Business Rules
- may purchase several **products**
- may never buy a **product** (but must have requested something that was unavailable)
- may make several **payments** for **products** purchased
- may never make a **payment** for a **product** (e.g., didn't buy anything; returned a defective product)

Data Attributes
- customer name
- customer email address
- customer account #
- credit card type (mv)
- credit card # (mv)
- card expiry date (mv)

Unique Identifier
Customer-ID

Pointers to Related Objects
Payment-ID (mv)
Video-ID (mv)

Fig. 2.22: Object Description – "Customer"

group. In the process "**Receive Payment**" (Fig. 2.21) we find that a customer can pay for a video, potentially at different times. Since we must track how each payment is made, we must include the data attributes *credit card type*, *credit card #* and *card expiry date*, and each must be multi-valued (mv) to support the different credit cards the customer uses.

To apply Business Data Rule # 5, the multi-valued items found in **CUSTOMER** that belong to a common group (*credit card type*, *credit card #* and *card expiry date*) are removed from the Parent Object (**CUSTOMER**) to establish a new Object (**CREDIT CARD**) that is characteristic of its Parent.

By taking repeating groups of data out of an Object (such as the above *credit card type*, *credit card #* and *card expiry date*, which are all multi-valued) and creating a new Object with the data, we are able to ask the client more precise and better focused questions (which we'll look at in detail when we get to the **Business Rules Table**, in the next chapter). In this example (Fig. 2.23), we are now able to ask the client questions about the specific type of payment made by the customer (the credit card), not just the payment in general. This increased granularity gives us better knowledge about the process of paying for the video, and how that payment is made.

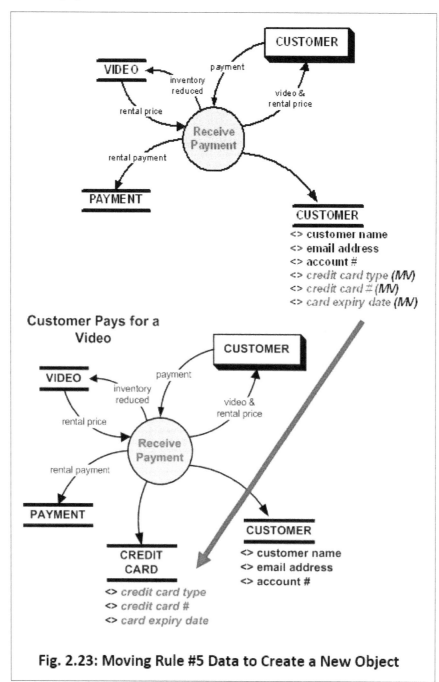

Fig. 2.23: Moving Rule #5 Data to Create a New Object

Note that the data items we moved from **CUSTOMER** to create the Object **CREDIT CARD** – *credit card type*, *credit card #* and *card expiry date* – are no longer multi-valued when they are used to create the **CREDIT CARD** Object. That's because each Object is seen as a single instance or occurrence of the thing it represents; i.e., it is a single **CREDIT CARD** record. In other words, each **PAYMENT** is made with a single, specific **CREDIT CARD** by the **CUSTOMER**.

Once you have internalized the **5 Business Data Rules** you will find yourself automatically removing multi-valued groups of data to form new Characteristic Objects. You will find that you can do this literally as you speak with your clients and first determine the need for the Object (**CREDIT CARD** in this case) and as you discuss the need to know about the customer's payments at different times. Once you have had sufficient practice with this approach to business systems analysis you won't spend a lot of time thinking about it, you'll just do it. But you will also miss a few when you're working directly with the client. So, we suggest you carefully review each Object when the client is not around. Then just look for any multi-valued ("mv") group of data that can be pulled out to make a new Characteristic Object. It's that easy. And remember, a group must consist of at least two data attributes (Business Data Rule # 3).

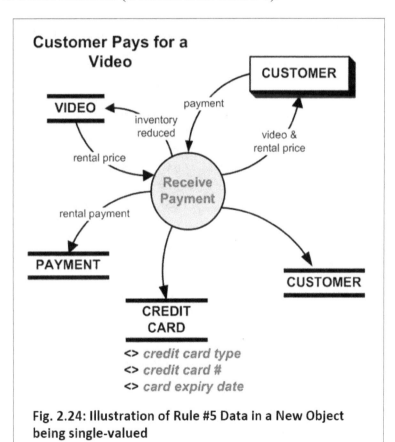

Fig. 2.24: Illustration of Rule #5 Data in a New Object being single-valued

Summary of the Business Data Rules

- **Business Data Rule # 1.** Attribute the data item to the Object it describes best, and to no other Object.

- **Business Data Rule # 2.** Each Object must have a unique identifier. The unique identifier must not be used as "data".

- **Business Data Rule # 3.** Each Object must have two or more data attributes, other than the unique identifier.

- **Business Data Rule # 4.** Any data item that is common to all subtypes of an Object must be attributed to that Object's supertype. Any data item that is attributed to one subtype Object cannot be attributed to another subtype Object.

- **Business Data Rule # 5.** When a repeating group of related data (multi-valued items) is found in a previously defined Object, create a new Object from the multi-valued data items found.

2.5 How to Determine if You Really Need a Data Item

As we discover Objects that are needed to support different business processes, we also find the nouns that are single data items, and we need to find a home for them. We attribute these data items to the right Objects by following the 5 Business Data Rules. But, data shouldn't be automatically accepted as necessary to support a business area or process just because someone mentions the data. In many cases data is included – just because it has always been there. The data item could be the legacy of a legacy system, but how do we find out if we still need the data that clients and subject-matter experts sometimes talk about?

Previously, we discussed how to apply the *Inclusion* and *Exclusion Questions (for Objects)*. We can do exactly the same thing with data items.

Ask the <u>Inclusion</u> Question (for Data).

Often when discussing a business process, different data items are mentioned by the client, but it's sometimes difficult to tell if all those data items are really necessary. How can we tell? One way to determine if a data item should be included is to ask the following question:

"If we know about {the data item} what will it <u>enable</u> us to do that we could not do if we didn't know about it?"

Let's look at an example using the *business event* "**It is Time to Deposit a Customer Payment to a Bank Account**".

Our subject-matter experts tell us that we need to keep track of the **PAYMENT**s that are **DEPOSIT**ed. We also need to know into which **BANK ACCOUNT** the payments are deposited; and, since there are many customers from coast-to-coast, we must know which **CUSTOMER** the deposited payment belongs to so we have a proper audit trail.

DEPOSIT

Data Attributes

- date of deposit
- name of depositor

As we listen to our client we are able to identify each of these as proper Objects (they all are nouns) which we recognized to consist of two or more data attributes … things we want to know about them. One of the data attributes belonging to the Object **DEPOSIT** is *date of deposit*. If we weren't sure this item was really needed, the first question would be, *is this really a necessary data item*? How can we tell? To find out let's restate the "Data Inclusion" question.

"If we know about {the date of deposit} **what will it enable us to do that we could not do if we didn't know about it?"**

In this example, *date of deposit* will allow us to reconcile our deposits against statements provided by the bank. Of course, that begs the question *do we want to reconcile deposits*? Is it within the scope of the project? Only our

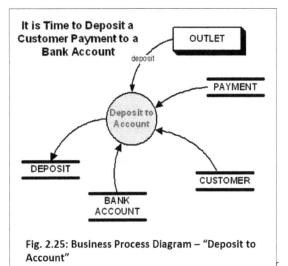

Fig. 2.25: Business Process Diagram – "Deposit to Account"

client knows for sure. If the answer is… *yes, reconciliation is within the scope of the project*… then we definitely need to know about the *date of deposit*.

Also, if reconciliation is within the scope of the project we must ask the question, *have we identified a business event for reconciliation yet*? If not, then we must add a new *business event*, "**It is Time to Reconcile Bank Statement**".

Ask the Exclusion Question (for Data).

There is another side of the 'Data Inclusion' question. Sometimes it makes more sense to try to take something away than to imagine it being added. This is the same as the 'Data Inclusion' test, but we're just coming at it from the other direction. In this case, the question we ask is stated as follows:

"If we do not know about {the data item} **what will it prevent us from doing that we must be able to do?"**

Let's use the same example as before, "**It is Time to Deposit Customer Payment to a Bank Account**".

"**If we <u>do not</u> know about {the date of deposit} what will it <u>prevent</u> us from doing that we must be able to do?**"

In this example (as in the previous one) it will prevent us from reconciling our deposits against statements received from the bank. Once again we have the same questions, *do we want to reconcile deposits*? Is it within the scope of the project? If the answer is… *yes, reconciliation is within the scope of the project*… then we must have the *date of deposit*.

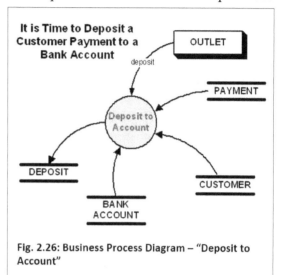

As with the 'Data Inclusion' test, we must add a new *business event* to be able to deal with "**It is Time to Reconcile Bank Statement**".

People have different views of things. That's why we have developed the 'Inclusion' and 'Exclusion' tests, so your clients will have the opportunity of seeing the subject from their own point of

Fig. 2.26: Business Process Diagram – "Deposit to Account"

view – whether something is enabled, or it is prevented – which helps to make the questions clear to them; not just to the analysts, but to the client. It's always a matter of perspective. Some people are more comfortable answering questions that exclude rather than include. It's probably that left-brain vs. right-brain thing.

Ask the <u>Inclusion</u> or <u>Exclusion</u> Questions (for Reports).

This is one of my personal favorites.

Here we are, well into the 21st century, but so many people still want to see reports being the primary output of systems. A report, of course, if a solution to some question – it's a *how* are we going to provide certain information, in some context.

DEPOSIT
<u>Data Attributes</u>
• date of deposit
• name of depositor

Rather than trying to tell your clients or SMEs that true business analysis doesn't address "how" something is done (such as issuing a report) but focuses on what is required to meet a need – which really means the essential data, not how it is delivered – it's best to find out the reason the client needs the report.

If the client says, *"We need a sales report for widgets in the northeast region"* we can ask either or both of the Inclusion and Exclusion Questions, as follows:

"If we <u>do not</u> know about {<u>the sales results for the northeast region</u>} what will it <u>prevent</u> us from doing that we must be able to do?"

Or ....

"If we know about {<u>the sales results for the northeast region</u>} what will it <u>enable</u> us to do that we could not do if we didn't know about it?"

The client's answer to either question can then be translated into a *business event* – a situation or circumstance that the system has to deal with.

There you have it: An effective way of using a request for a report to determine what the real *business event* may be.

Chapter 3. The Business Rules Table – How to Find the Questions to Ask

Contents

The single most difficult issue for any consultant when doing business analysis has always been finding the right questions to ask clients and subject-matter experts (SMEs). The consultant's quandry has always been, *How do I know what I should ask these people? What should my first question be? And what should I ask next?*

Every business and system analysis methodology has always lacked this fundamental foundation – a method to find the exact, in-context questions to ask clients and SMEs. The only way we can be assured of the completeness of any business requirements specification is to somehow know that we have asked all the right questions, and none have been missed. Anything less makes not a business system specification, but a business *speculation*. Business requirements analysis isn't horseshoes. *"Close is good enough"* just isn't acceptable for the sophisticated, integrated, expensive business systems we need to have today.

The Kinds of Questions

Agile business analysis means nothing if we can't find all the correct questions to ask our stakeholders. It's not "agile" to leave unasked, and unanswered, questions on the floor. Therefore, to be able to start and finish business requirements analysis for any project, all of the following questions must be answered or resolved.

1. **How do I find all the right questions to ask?** How do I quickly find all the questions to ask our clients and SMEs? How do I know what the questions should be? (The operative words here are *find*, *all* and *quickly*.)

2. **How do I know all the right questions have been asked?** How do I find unanswered questions? How do I find the ones no one ever seems to find, or the ones we promised to come back to later and need to keep track of? How do I know we're done? How do I know we have found <u>all</u> the questions that need to be asked? (In other words, how can I know what I don't know?)

3. **How do I find the real limits of the project?** How do I find the questions that determine the real scope of the project? How do I prevent 'scope creep' during the project? How do I avoid surprises? (Or, how can I turn the scope issue into something real rather than trying to pin Jell-O to a wall?)

4. **How do I create a small, understandable and business-focused requirements document that everyone can understand?** How can I put all the related documentation in the same place, without redundancy, so I can find it again? How do I make the documentation brief, event-based, and not like a Victorian novel, so we can easily maintain it and find elements? How can I write it in business language, and not base it on the technology we're implementing? How can I make sure it focuses on the business and not on the technology solution? (And, how can we release and distribute in an "agile" fashion using modern media?)

5. **How do I describe data access requirements based on the business needs?** If we need a database design, how can I quickly determine the data accesses required by the business needs, so database designers don't have to go out and reinvent the business wheel? (And how can I, as an analyst and not a database designer, do this magic?)

3.1 How to Find the Questions to Ask Clients

All of the questions listed above can be answered and resolved by using the questions outlined in Chapter 2, the *Inclusion / Exclusion Questions* and the **Business Rules Table**, which we will discuss now.

- The **Business Rules Table** (BRT) is a question generator. It requires a specific syntax – a *language of structure* – so we can ask questions of clients and SMEs. This syntax eliminates personal and subjective evaluations of whether a question (or answer) is a 'good' one. All BRT-generated questions, and all answers from clients, have an equal value. This means we never have to be concerned with someone else's intuitive understanding.

- The **Business Rules Table** enables the analyst to easily identify and structure all questions to be asked about the business domain, in the context of specific business processes.

- The **<u>Business Rules Table</u>** enables the analyst to write a clear statement for the desired business policy, in plain language, in the context of a specific business process.

- The **<u>Business Rules Table</u>** enables the analyst to know where to document the client's answer, and to know where to find the answer in the future.

- The **<u>Business Rules Table</u>** enables the business analyst to find *business events* (conditions, situations and circumstances) the client did not recognize to be part of the project's scope, and therefore the supporting business processes that would otherwise be missed.

- The **<u>Business Rules Table</u>** enables the analyst to know when there are no more questions to ask the client about the project's business requirements.

The resulting documentation, written in plain and simple business language, can be easily read and evaluated by the client or subject-matter experts. The succinctness of the documentation enables SMEs to evaluate individual business processes and to determine if any new processes and data effectively contribute to the organization's mission, goals and direction.

Governing business rules, which come from the questions generated by the **<u>Business Rules Table</u>**, are the rules or policies that govern the existence or behavior of {the Object we are questioning}, <u>in the context of a specific business process</u>. Everything we learn about an Object is documented as a set of rules that govern the client's business, <u>in a specific circumstance</u>. These rules become the key part of the business requirements specification. They represent functionality and required (or denied) behavior in a specific situation.

Each Object that is part of a process supporting a *business event* (Fig. 3.1) becomes part of a matrix called the **<u>Business Rules Table</u>**. The symbols used in the BRT (see Fig. 3.2) are shorthand notation for specific answers to the questions that are asked. Although the BRT contains the shorthand notation, the actual context-specific rules are documented in plain language, using declarative statements.

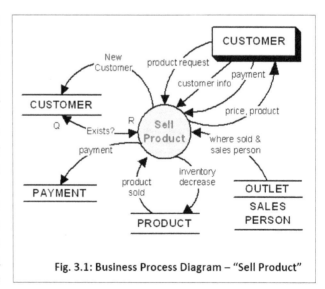

Fig. 3.1: Business Process Diagram – "Sell Product"

Symbols used in the **<u>Business Rules Table</u>** to symbolize this shorthand, also known as *ratio of occurrences* (or cardinality), are shown in Fig. 3.2.

1	=	One only
N	=	Numerous (more than one)
0	=	None (means "never")
NA	=	Does not apply (= 0 [zero] occurrences)

Fig. 3.2: Notation for Business Rules Table (BRT)

Using a *language of structure* to ask questions of clients results in business rules specific to a process. These business rules are documented, as declarative statements, also specific to a business process.

From a data perspective, a process can also be seen as a relationship among Objects, behaving in a specific context.

A **<u>Business Rules Table</u>** is produced for each **Business Process Diagram**. An example of the completed **<u>Business Rules Table</u>** for the process "**Sell Product**" is shown in Fig. 3.3. The business process "**Sell Product**" supports the *business event* "**The Customer Buys a Product**".

BRT	Salesperson	Customer	Outlet	Product	Payment
1 Salesperson		N,0	1,N	N,0	N,0
1 Customer	1,N,0		1,N	1,N,0	1,N,0
1 Outlet	N	N		N	N
1 Product	1,N,0	1,N,0	1,N		1,N,0
1 Payment	1,N	1	1	1,N	

These are the 'Anchor' Objects.

Fig. 3.3: Business Rules Table – "Sell Product"

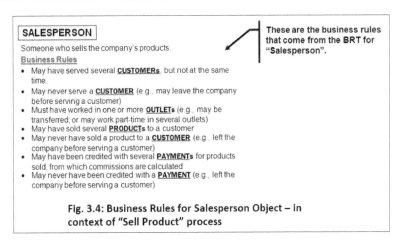

Fig. 3.4: Business Rules for Salesperson Object – in context of "Sell Product" process

Business Rules Table questions have a *language of structure* to get good answers. "Good" means nothing less than complete and accurate. Each Object must be queried with three (3) specific questions to uncover all the business rules relevant to the specific process in which it participates, <u>and</u> to be able to find other *business events* required to support the target business area. Below is an example of the type of rules that would result from the table entries shown in Fig. 3.3 for the Object <u>SALESPERSON</u>. The rule notation in Fig. 3.3 is read from left to right, and translates into the text in Fig. 3.4.

	BRT	Salesperson	Customer	Outlet	Product	Payment
1	**Salesperson**		N,0	1,N	N,0	N,0
1	**Customer**	1,N,0		1,N	1,N,0	1,N,0
1	**Outlet**	N	N		N	N
1	**Product**	1,N,0	1,N,0	1,N		1,N,0
1	**Payment**	1,N	1	1	1,N	

These are the 'Anchor' Objects.

Fig. 3.3: Business Rules Table – "Sell Product"

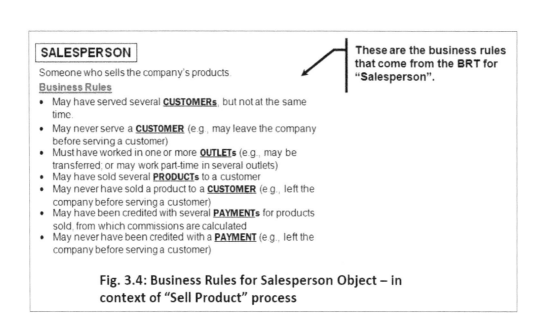

SALESPERSON

Someone who sells the company's products.

Business Rules

- May have served several **CUSTOMERs**, but not at the same time.
- May never serve a **CUSTOMER** (e.g., may leave the company before serving a customer)
- Must have worked in one or more **OUTLETs** (e.g., may be transferred; or may work part-time in several outlets)
- May have sold several **PRODUCTs** to a customer
- May never have sold a product to a **CUSTOMER** (e.g., left the company before serving a customer)
- May have been credited with several **PAYMENTs** for products sold, from which commissions are calculated
- May never have been credited with a **PAYMENT** (e.g., left the company before serving a customer)

These are the business rules that come from the BRT for "Salesperson".

Fig. 3.4: Business Rules for Salesperson Object – in context of "Sell Product" process

Each Object is placed in the **Business Rules Table** twice – once as an entry in the row on the left and once in a column at the top. We add Objects to the table only as they are discovered when we determine the Objects necessary to support a business process. An Object can intersect or *join* with several other Objects in the table. It is not possible that an Object never joins with any other Object. While it is possible that a single Object can be alone in a specific process, it must join with at least one other Object when all the **Business Rules Table**s are combined for the purpose of database design.

We start at the first row on the left with the first Object.

We start here with the first 'anchor' Object.

BRT	Salesperson	Customer	Outlet
1 Salesperson			
1 Customer			
1 Outlet			

Fig. 3.5: Business Rules Table – Where to Start

We then ask questions about Objects that appear in a specific **Business Process Diagram**. (We'll visit what the specific questions are in a moment.) We ask our questions of only two Objects at one time ... in binary pairs, if you like. This enables us to ask a series of stable questions and get specific, stable answers.

Fig. 3.6: Business Process Diagram – "Sell Product"

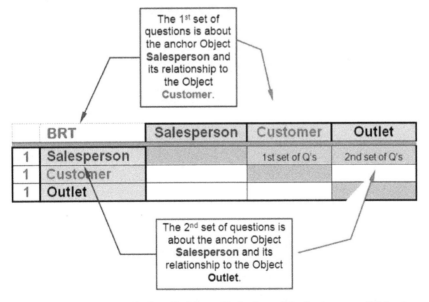

The 1st set of questions is about the anchor Object Salesperson and its relationship to the Object Customer.

BRT	Salesperson	Customer	Outlet
1 Salesperson		1st set of Q's	2nd set of Q's
1 Customer			
1 Outlet			

The 2nd set of questions is about the anchor Object Salesperson and its relationship to the Object Outlet.

Fig. 3.7: Business Rules Table – Relationship between Objects

So, how does this work? Let's work through an example using just three of the Objects identified in the **Business Process Diagram** for "Sell Product".

Fig. 3.8: Business Rules Table – "Sell Product"

From the process "**Sell Product**", place the Objects in the **Business Rules Table** – once in a row on the left, and once in a column across the top. Place the number "**1**" in front of each anchor Object. This will help us focus on a single instance of the anchor Object when we ask the questions that arise from this table. (I did not place all of the Objects from the "**Sell Product**" process into the BRT, just to conserve some space.)

We start with the first anchor Object, and we structure the questions as follows:

Structure: "For a single, specific {<u>anchor OBJECT</u>} how many {<u>intersecting OBJECTs</u>} might {<u>verb construct</u>}?"

Let's put that into an English-language structure we can all understand.

"For a single, specific SALESPERSON how many CUSTOMERs might he or she serve?"

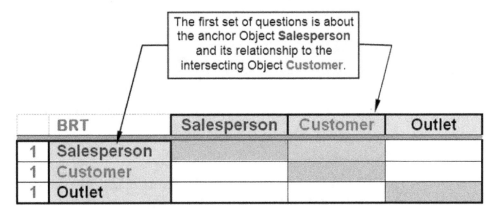

Fig. 3.9: Business Rules Table – First set of questions

The questions that come from this table must always be put into a context. The context is the verb you chose. For example, what do salespersons do in the "**Sell Product**" process? They **sell to** or **serve** customers. In this example, then, the context must be something like the verb ***to serve*** or ***to sell***. I have chosen ***to serve*** since it seems easier to work with. Words like "associated" or "related" should never be used since they are far too abstract and only have meaning to the person using them.

This initial question is only intended to help us focus our thinking. Never attempt to answer the first, general question. It's just a mental placeholder, so we can get on with the more specific questions. We immediately follow this initial question with three very specific questions, each soliciting a clear and unambiguous answer.

QUESTION # 1:

Structure: "Could the {anchor OBJECT} {relationship context verb} just one {intersecting OBJECT}?"

Or, in plain English:

"Could the SALESPERSON serve just one CUSTOMER?"

QUESTION # 2:

Structure: "Could the {anchor OBJECT} {relationship context verb} several {intersecting OBJECTs}?"

Or, in plain English:

"Could the SALESPERSON serve several CUSTOMERs?"

QUESTION # 3:

Structure: "Might the {anchor OBJECT} never {relationship context verb} any {intersecting OBJECTs} at all?"

Or, in plain English:

"Might the SALESPERSON never serve any CUSTOMERs at all?"

So far, we have a total of four questions, except that the initial "placeholder" question doesn't require an answer.

PLACEHOLDER QUESTION:

"For a single, specific SALESPERSON how many CUSTOMERs might he or she serve?" (Do not wait for answer.)

This is followed immediately by three specific questions, each requiring a response from the client or subject matter expert.

	BRT	Salesperson	Customer	Outlet
1	**Salesperson**		?	
1	Customer			
1	Outlet			

Fig. 3.10: Business Rules Table – Questions in the intersection cell

QUESTION # 1: "Could the SALESPERSON serve just one CUSTOMER?"

QUESTION # 2: "Could the SALESPERSON serve several CUSTOMERs?"

QUESTION # 3: "Might the SALESPERSON never serve any CUSTOMERs at all?"

Each of these questions is asked in what we call a client-interactive "requirements *discovery* session". Discovery sessions with subject-matter experts are very similar to technical JAD sessions, but *discovery* sessions focus entirely on the business requirements and not on system solutions or design. **J**oint **A**pplication **D**esign (or Development) is a session in which subject-matter experts and system developers interact to determine system functionality and output. In business discovery sessions, answers to questions are captured by an expert scribe, based on the **Business Rules Table**s for each **Business Process Diagram**.

Let's play through the answers to our questions – we'll make up some answers along the way, pretending subject-matter experts are present – and populate the **Business Rules Table** with the values representing our made-up answers. From these answers we'll also generate plain-language text that documents the rules in Objects.

BRT	Salesperson	Customer	Outlet
1 **Salesperson**		?	
1 Customer			
1 Outlet			

Fig. 3.11: Business Rules Table – Questions in the intersection cell

Start with the **PLACEHOLDER QUESTION: "For a single, specific SALESPERSON how many CUSTOMERs might he or she serve?"** But don't wait for answer. Immediately go on with the three follow-on questions.

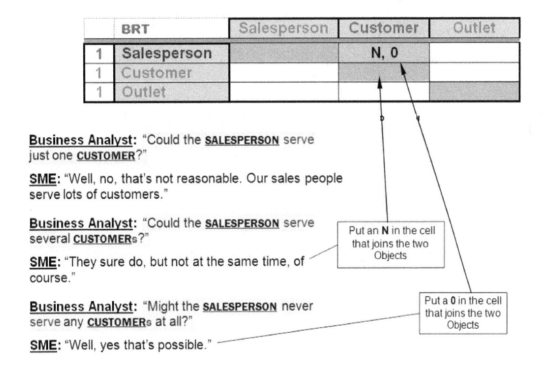

BRT	Salesperson	Customer	Outlet
1 **Salesperson**		N, 0	
1 Customer			
1 Outlet			

Business Analyst: "Could the **SALESPERSON** serve just one **CUSTOMER**?"

SME: "Well, no, that's not reasonable. Our sales people serve lots of customers."

Business Analyst: "Could the **SALESPERSON** serve several **CUSTOMER**s?"

SME: "They sure do, but not at the same time, of course."

Business Analyst: "Might the **SALESPERSON** never serve any **CUSTOMER**s at all?"

SME: "Well, yes that's possible."

Put an **N** in the cell that joins the two Objects

Put a **0** in the cell that joins the two Objects

Fig. 3.12: Business Rules Table – Questions to Answers: Salesperson-Customer

You will recall that earlier we reviewed the notation we use to record the ratio of occurrences between Objects. Ratio of occurrences, or cardinality, specifies how many instances (or occurrences) of an intersecting Object there are for a single anchor Object. Now, by itself, that's not very interesting information, and it doesn't seem to have much to do with business requirements analysis. But the moment we put that into the context of a business process, then we've defined the nature of the relationship between the intersecting Objects, and we can define the rules of that relationship, as specified by our subject-matter experts. As a consultant, you don't have to agree with the rules the SMEs specify; but you do have to accept that they know more about their business than we do. I've repeated the notation so we can all work from the same page.

1	=	One only
N	=	Numerous (more than one)
0	=	None (means "never")
NA	=	Does not apply (= 0 [zero] occurrences)

Fig. 3.13: Notation for Business Rules Table (BRT)

By revisiting the 3rd Question we find that the SME gave us a technically correct but not very enlightening answer:

Business Analyst: "Might the **SALESPERSON** never serve any **CUSTOMER**s at all?"

SME: "Well, yes that's possible."

With this answer, we enter a "**0**" in the **Business Rules Table** cell (at the intersection of **SALESPERSON** and **CUSTOMER**) but we must go on to a follow-on question.

Business Analyst's Follow-on Question: "Under what circumstances might that be true – that they might never serve a customer?"

SME: "Well, they could leave the company before serving their first customer."

Whenever there is a "never" response from a client, such as above, you must always ask one additional question – "**Under what circumstances might that be true?**" This is the final Question and is only asked when the client responds to the 3rd Question with "never".

Each of the rules you have now discovered must also be documented in plain language. This isn't difficult, especially since you have already selected the context (verb construct) that you will use. Let's review the questions (and answers) in our example.

> **Business Analyst's 1st Question:** "Could the **SALESPERSON** serve just one **CUSTOMER**?"
>
> **SME:** "Well, no, that's not reasonable. Our sales people serve lots of customers."

Since the answer was "no" then there is nothing to add to the **Business Rules Table** and nothing to write up as the business rule.

> **Business Analyst's 2nd Question:** "Could the **SALESPERSON** serve several **CUSTOMERs**?"
>
> **SME:** "They sure do, but not at the same time, of course."

With this answer we now know that a salesperson may serve many customers, since serving none is not a reasonable scenario. With this answer we enter **"N"** in the cell that joins **SALESPERSON** with **CUSTOMER**.

BRT		Salesperson	Customer	Outlet
1	**Salesperson**		N	
1	Customer			
1	Outlet			

Fig. 3.14: Notation for Business Rules Table (BRT)

We then write the rule in plain language under the 'anchor' Object (**SALESPERSON**). The rule can be written as *"may have served several customers, but not at the same time"*. When we use 'may' as in "may have served several customers" we are also implying the salesperson "may not have served several customers". Therefore, before we choose 'may' instead of 'must' it's important to know the answer to the next question, since the words we choose to write our rules do have precise meanings.

SALESPERSON

Someone who sells the company's products.

Business Rules
- May have served several **CUSTOMERs**, but not at the same time
- May never serve a **CUSTOMER**

Data Attributes
- salesperson name
- salesperson address
- salesperson phone # (mv)
- salesperson fax #
- salesperson email address (mv)

Unique Identifier
Salesperson-ID

Fig. 3.15: Object Business Rules

Business Analyst's 3rd Question: Might the SALESPERSON never serve any CUSTOMERs at all?"

SME: "Well, yes they could."

With this answer we also place a **"0"** (zero) in the cell that joins SALESPERSON with CUSTOMER. The rule can be written as *"may never serve a customer"*.

BRT	Salesperson	Customer	Outlet
1 Salesperson		N, 0	
1 Customer			
1 Outlet			

Fig. 3.16: Notation for Business Rules Table (BRT)

Whenever we get a "never" response to this 3rd question we must ask a fourth follow-on question to determine the condition that makes it true.

Business Analyst's 4th Question: "Under what circumstances might that be true?"

SME: "Well, they could leave the company before serving their first customer."

In this case, because we got a "never" response to the 4th question, we must qualify the business rule we previously recorded. In this case we take the original rule (*"may never serve a customer"*) and add (*e.g., may leave the company before serving a customer*). As with the original statement, this rule is allocated to the anchor Object SALESPERSON.

Whenever a "never" response is given by a client, they must support the "never" condition with an example (or several). In turn, you must determine if the circumstances identified in the example is *a business event that has not yet been included* in the project's scope... and if so, is it in-scope or out-of-scope?

In the example we are using, the example states that the salesperson may leave the company. The

SALESPERSON

Someone who sells the company's products.

Business Rules
- May have served several CUSTOMERs, but not at the same time
- May never serve a CUSTOMER (e.g., may leave the company before serving a customer)

Data Attributes
- salesperson name
- salesperson address
- salesperson phone # (mv)
- salesperson fax #
- salesperson email address (mv)

Unique Identifier
Salesperson-ID

Fig. 3.17: Object Business Rules with example of "never" response to 4th BRT Question

question you must therefore ask the client is, "*Is this something – the salesperson may leave the company before serving a customer – that we want to keep track of?*"

The simple fact that a SME mentioned the example – stimulated by our question – forces us to consider its inclusion. If the SME's answer is "*yes, it's something we want to keep track of*" we must add it to our parking lot of *business events* that make up the project's scope – perhaps listed as "**The Employee Terminates**" (quits, dies, retires). If the client's answer is "*no, it's not part of the scope*" then we won't include it – although we do keep track of *business events* found to be out-of-scope as well. (This gives us a good audit or management trail.) However, it's not usual for a SME to use an example of a situation that could arise, and then say it's not something they want to know about. That's OK. But, in the end, it's either in or it's out.

I have found it is easier to get a response when asking if "we want to keep track of" something, rather than "Is this within the project's scope?" Earlier, we discussed how all systems just keep track of things. (If you don't keep track of something, you can't know about it.) Therefore, if the client wants to "keep track of" something, it means it's inside scope. This is also why so many projects are called "XYZ Tracking Project".

Also, two *business event* lists are maintained – one for **In-Scope Business Events** and another for **Out-of-Scope Business Events**. This enables us to keep track of those *business events* that were discussed but determined to be out-of-scope. The out-of-scope *business events* could become in-scope on a future project. By keeping track we're also able to answer questions such as, "did you discuss ....?"

The 4th BRT Question is a primary method used to discover *business events* that are within a project's scope. That's why it is so important to listen carefully to what clients and subject-matter experts have to say, especially to their "never" answers, and to get the circumstances that make the "never" responses true.

This procedure of asking 3 or 4 specific questions (which we simply call the 'BRT Questions') is repeated for all the Objects that intersect with the anchor Object **SALESPERSON**. After we have finished asking questions of all the Objects that have a relationship with **SALESPERSON** – specific to a process – then we go on to the next anchor Object, which is **CUSTOMER** in our example.

BRT		Salesperson	Customer	Outlet
1	Salesperson		N, 0	1, N
1	Customer			
1	Outlet			

These are the 'Anchor' Objects.

Fig. 3.18: Business Rules Table (BRT) – Relationships between Objects

Because there are three very specific questions (and sometimes a fourth) you will never fumble trying to figure out what the questions should be or what comes next. You will find the 'BRT Questions' procedure to be very fast and effective. And you will find that your clients relate to these questions very well. They sometimes struggle to answer, but that's because the questions are so specific and call for a precise answer. Many interesting discussions and policies come out of these questions.

Where do we put the rules? All rules are allocated to and documented under the Object that is the 'anchor' Object in the question.

And when we're all done we have all kinds of business rules attributed to all the Objects that we need to support a specific process. Our limited example, **SALESPERSON**, would look something like the entry in Fig. 3.19. I didn't go through the entire table with all the Objects since that would simply take too long. We will play through a more complete example later.

And how do we go about asking the 'BRT Questions' of all the Objects that are part of a business process, so we can find all the rules?

Immediately upon completing a **Business Process Diagram** we start asking the 'BRT Questions' of our clients. As a result, we gain an understanding of the business rules in a specific context (a process) right away, which enables us to progressively understand better each answer we get from our clients. This approach also enables us to learn incrementally, which means that we don't have to start the project with a whole lot of knowledge.

SALESPERSON
Someone who sells the company's products.
Business Rules
• May have served several **CUSTOMER**s, but not at the same time
• May never serve a **CUSTOMER** (e.g., may leave the company before serving a customer)
• Must have worked in one or more **OUTLET**s (may be transferred or may work part-time in several outlets)
Data Attributes
• salesperson name
• salesperson address
• salesperson phone # (mv)
• salesperson fax #
• salesperson email address (mv)
Unique Identifier
Salesperson-ID

Fig. 3.19: Object with Business Rules

3.2 The Value of Asking the Questions

It's important to recognize that analysis is all about asking questions … and thus finding the answers. The ability to do this quickly, without spinning wheels, is a function of asking the right questions, in context, the very first time. It's not about getting the answers from ourselves (and out of our own head) based on our hypothetical understanding of the client's business system, without ever talking to the client and subject-matter experts. It's about getting down with the clients and SMEs, and asking them all the relevant questions that have to be asked. And, it's about doing it quickly and effectively.

Sadly, many business system analysts – experienced ones and brand new ones – think it takes too much time to ask all the required questions of clients and SMEs. So they don't. The interesting thing about all the precise questions that come out of the individual **Business Rules Table**s is that … they actually help us get the work done faster than by not asking the questions. The questions identified by the individual **Business Rules Table**s focus on nothing but the rules of behavior between one group of data and another (i.e., Objects), in a context where these data comes together. It doesn't get any tighter or more concise than that.

How many times have clients gone off on tangents that appear to have little to do with the objectives of the project? How many times have teams experienced loss of focus in meetings or client-interactive sessions? How often have we heard the refrain, *"my client doesn't know what they want"*? All of these challenges can be attributed to meetings without a way of keeping everyone in focus and on target. And all of these challenges take time, time, time. It is simply faster and much more effective to go directly to the questions to be asked, ask them, and get immediate answers in variations of "yes", "no", "maybe" or "sometimes" – all of which can be decoded. Even though there may be scores of questions to ask our clients, it's a whole lot faster and better to know exactly what the questions are than to have to meander through the business analysis without focus. The other benefit is that you know when the entire job is done. It's not a guess. You know.

So, how fast can it get? Well, let's remember that any charlatan can finish faster than you simply by <u>not</u> doing some of the work required. But to know that the work is absolutely complete *<u>and</u>* it was finished fast, that's another matter. And that truly is "agile". I will give you a metric later in the book when we discuss how long it takes to complete a *discovery session* and the ensuing work, so we can have a measurable definition of "fast".

I mentioned earlier that at the center of their being most systems do just one thing: They keep track of stuff, so we can find the "stuff" later – or use it to make new "stuff". Therefore, based on the principle of finding the answer first and then discovering the question, it is the business analyst's job to discover what the client needs *to find*, and under what circumstances. By finding the circumstances (the *business events*) we can identify what it is we need to know, and therefore identify what we need to record or remember.

So what does all of this accomplish? By asking the questions generated by Object relationships in the BRT, it enables the following:

- It enables us to quickly find the specific business rules that determine required and disallowed behavior in a specific context.
- It enables us to find *business events* that had not yet been mentioned by the clients, and have not yet been discovered.

- It enables us to find Objects and data attributes that we need which have not yet been discovered.

- Based on discovering new *business events* (via the 4th 'BRT Question'), we may discover new Objects not previously defined; therefore we will discover new data attributes and new business rules too.)

- It enables us to eliminate scope creep due to errors of omission – things we didn't know to ask about, or our clients didn't think to tell us about.

The rules that come from the 'BRT Questions'– always in the singular context of a specific *business event* (a circumstance, condition or situation) – are a different way of prescribing the behavior of the system, from an exclusive business context. Therefore, the **Business Process Diagrams** (and accompanying text), along with Object definitions and the rules derived from the 'BRT Questions' eliminate the need for other behavior models at the business specification level. That reduces the amount of work needed considerably, but no facts or business requirements are missed. This is, at least in my definition of the universe, truly agile. (Yes, I will discuss how long this takes later.)

Also, all of the business rules that come from the 'BRT Questions' lead directly to test cases.

Each business rule is a clear (and brief) contextual specification of required (or denied) behavior. A test case of functionality can be easily built around each of these business rule statement. Since this is done up-front as part of the business discovery, it eliminates the need to spend an lot of time figuring out business functionality later; thus, more time is saved, and "agile" business analysis takes on more meaning.

3.3 How to Write Clear Business Rules

By asking the 'BRT Questions' we can easily generate all the business rules needed for the project and the affected business areas, with each rule stated in a specific context. Each of the business rules is constructed from the responses we get after asking the 'BRT Questions', and all rules are written in plain language. Each rule is attributed and documented under the anchor Object that forms part of the 'BRT Question'. An example of how rules are attributed to an Object (**SALESPERSON**) is illustrated in Fig. 3.21, based on the limited **Business Rules Table** (Fig. 3.20).

	BRT	Salesperson	Customer	Outlet
1	Salesperson		N, 0	1, N
1	Customer			
1	Outlet			

Fig. 3.20: Business Rules Table – Salesperson Relationships

Business rules should be written as simple, single-subject declarative statements. This helps the reader understand exactly what we mean when we document the rules, and we never have to rely on someone else's comprehension of the language or their intuitive understanding.

The 'BRT Questions' we ask our clients solicit clear, unambiguous answers, which can only be *"yes," "no"* or *"sometimes"* and *"maybe"* (which we'll get to soon). We use shorthand (e.g., 0, 1, or N) to note our clients' answers, and we call this shorthand **multiplicity** or **cardinality** or, better stated, *the ratio of occurrences between the anchor Object and its intersecting Objects*. The ratio of occurrences that's entered in the cell that joins two Objects indicates how we should write the business rules.

SALESPERSON
Someone who sells the company's products.

Business Rules
- May have served several **CUSTOMER**s, but not at the same time
- May never serve a **CUSTOMER** (e.g., may leave the company before serving a customer)
- Must have worked in one or more **OUTLET**s (may be transferred or may work part-time in several outlets)

Data Attributes
- salesperson name
- salesperson address
- salesperson phone # (mv)
- salesperson fax #
- salesperson email address (mv)

Unique Identifier
Salesperson-ID

Fig. 3.21: Object with Business Rules

For example:

- If there is a **1** only we write, "**must be only one** {**OBJECT**}" as the business rule statement.

- If there is a value of **1, N** only we write, "**must be one or more** {**OBJECTs**}" as the business rule statement.

- If there is a value of **N** only we write, "**must be several** {**OBJECTs**}" as the business rule statement.

- If there is a value of **1, N, 0** we write, "**must be one or more** {**OBJECTs**} ... **unless there are none**"; or we can write "**may be several** {**OBJECTs**} ... **unless there are none**" as the business rule statement. We can also write two rules for the **1, N, 0** relationship, such as "**may be one or more** {**OBJECTs**}" ..." followed by "**may never be an** {**OBJECT**}...".

- If there is a value of **N, 0** we write "**must be more than one** {**OBJECT**} ... **unless there are none**"; or we can write "**must be several** {**OBJECTs**} ... **unless there are none**" as the business rule statement.

- If there is a **0** value we write "**will never have an** {**OBJECT**}..." as a separate business rule statement.

In all of the above I have used the relationship verb "to be" or "to have" to join the anchor and intersecting Objects. Below, there are examples of these rules, written in plain language, with verb constructs other than the generic "to be".

- If there is a **1** only we can write, under the **CUSTOMER** Object, "**must receive only one PAYMENT**" as the business rule statement.

BRT	Customer	Payment
1	Customer		1
1	Payment		

Fig. 3.22: BRT Object with "1" entry

- If there is a value of **1, N** we can write, under the **CUSTOMER** Object, "**must receive one or more PAYMENTs**" as the business rule statement.

BRT	Customer	Payment
1	Customer		1, N
1	Payment		

Fig. 3.23: BRT Object with "1,N" entry

- If there is a value of **N** only we can write, under the **CUSTOMER** Object, "**must receive several PAYMENTs**" as the business rule statement.

BRT	Customer	Payment
1	Customer		N
1	Payment		

Fig. 3.24: BRT Object with "N" entry

- If there is a value of **1, N, 0** we can write, "**must receive one or more PAYMENTs ... unless there are none**"; or we can write "**may receive several PAYMENTs ... unless there are none**" as the business rule statement. We can also write two rules for the **1, N, 0** relationship, such as "**may receive one or more PAYMENTs**" ..." followed by "**may never receive a PAYMENT...**".

BRT	Customer	Payment
1	Customer		1, N, 0
1	Payment		

Fig. 3.25: BRT Object with "1,N,0" entry

- If there is a value of **N, 0** we can write "**must receive more than one PAYMENT ... unless there are none**"; or we can write "**must receive several PAYMENTs ... unless there are none**" as the business rule statement.

BRT	Customer	Payment
1	Customer		N, 0
1	Payment		

Fig. 3.26: BRT Object with "N,0" entry

- If there is a **0** value only, we write "**will never receive a PAYMENT...**" as a separate business rule statement.

BRT		Customer	Payment
1	Customer		0
1	Payment		

Fig. 3.27: BRT Object with "0" entry

As you can imagine, it's very important to be precise (i.e., *exact, as in measurement or amount*) and concise (i.e., *expressing much in few words*) when writing the business rules. The shorthand notation of 1, N and 0 tells us just about everything, but it doesn't put the relationship in the context of a chosen verb construct. Therefore, we write out the rule in plain language, joining the two related Objects in a relationship described by the chosen verb. While the simple cardinality of 1, N and 0 may be enough for database designers, the business folks need to see the rule written out clearly, in plain business language.

3.4 How to Find Complementary Business Events

The *business event* is the foundation for all business processes. In other words, if there is no situation or circumstance to deal with (which is how we define a *business event*) then there is no need for a process. Finding *business event*, then, is the most important job of all.

Most *business events* have complementary *business events* – counterparts. Some *business events* must have opposite ends and predecessor and subsequent *business events*, or the project would not be complete in its logical coverage. Finding these is not a strange journey to a mysterious land. All we have to do is to identify the complementary, opposite, predecessor or subsequent *business event* and then ask the client if it is a *situation* or *circumstance* that they want to keep track of. A couple of examples of questions you might want to ask to determine *business events* that fall into these categories follow.

- You have identified the *business event* "**The Customer Buys a Product**" as being within the scope of your project. Does the complementary *business event* "**The Customer Returns a Product**" also fall inside the scope of the project? Are these returns something you want to keep track of?

- "**It is Time to Order a Product from a Supplier**" has been identified as a *business event* inside your project's scope. Does the subsequent *business event* "**The Product Arrives from the Supplier**" also belong to the project? Do you want to keep track of products that arrive from suppliers?

- "**A Vendor Applies for Approval to be a Recognized Vendor**" has been identified as a *business event* inside your project's scope. Do the related *business events* "**The Vendor is Suspended**" and "**The Vendor Ceases Operation**" also belong to the project? Do you want to keep track of suspended vendors or vendors that cease operations?

As we discussed earlier, the "keep track of" question is far better to use than asking if something is inside a project's scope. Asking about scope is a bit abstract for most people (notice how they scrunch their eyebrows as they think about this), whereas asking "do you want to keep track of xyz" becomes a whole lot easier to deal with.

Finding these complementary or related *business events* is making sure we ask the client all the follow-on questions that come as a result of discovering other *business events*. Finding the opposite end of a *business event* is making sure nothing is left unasked. Finding these complementary *business events* is establishing the limits to the project by stepping out to its perimeter and beyond and then determining where the scope line comes to rest. Scope creep will always be a challenge unless there is some way to determine the limits to the project. You can use the **Business Rules Table** and the 'BRT Questions' to determine what's in and what's out, but you also need to look for the complementary *business events* that make up the whole.

3.5 Good Questions are Closed-Ended

Open-ended questions are good for stimulating discussion but not so good for getting clear and specific answers. Therefore we rarely ask open-ended questions like, *"what do we need to know about customers?"* Not only will an answer take a long time, but we have no reasonable hope of achieving specific answers with such a question. This kind of question, while it might create interesting discussion, really just transfers the responsibility for analysis from the business analyst to the client or subject-matter expert. Most (but not all) open-ended questions do not lend anything of value to "agile" business analysis. Instead, we have to ask simple and closed-ended questions about the data (Objects) that's needed to support a process. We do this with closed-ended questions through the **Business Rules Table** and the 'BRT Questions', which tends to encourage direct and unusually concise answers. They cause answers such as *"yes," "no"* and *"no, that's not what I mean."*

While I strongly support the idea of open-ended questions to stimulate discussion and brainstorming – which is sometimes very necessary – I equally strongly discourage this approach if the objective is to get concise answers to specific questions quickly. The idea of "agile" business analysis also means getting clear and concise answers to questions quickly. Since the 'BRT Questions' have a specific syntax, they are designed to elicit exact answers rapidly.

The idea of using closed-ended questions based on a specific predefined syntax also removes business system analysis from the realm of 'art', as so many have called it (an elitist idea, if I ever heard one). The 'art', as I understand it, has always been finding the questions to ask. And whoever was good at finding better questions – and therefore got better and faster answers – was considered to be the best and most experienced analyst. The **Business Rules Table** and the 'BRT Questions' enable all of us to become artists.

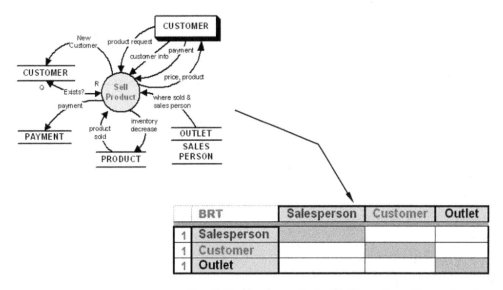

Fig. 3.28: Business Rules Table – Questions about Objects specific to a process

3.6 What to do when the Answer is "It depends ..."?

Sometimes, when we ask questions of clients or SMEs we get answers like "*well, it depends...*" or "*maybe*" or "*sometimes*". While these answers are often seen as frustratingly vague or evasive, and may even appear defensive, it's really quite the opposite.

Sometimes, in real life, the answer is ... "*it depends*". This is simply a conditional response; that is, under one circumstance the answer is "*no*", while under another circumstance the answer is "*yes*". You will recall that a *business event* is a "condition or circumstance ...." One of the two circumstances suggested by an 'it depends' type of answer is most likely a *business event* that you have already found, while the other one has not yet been discovered and added to your **Project Business Event List**. This kind of answer, then, is an opportunity to find a new *business event* that's not so obvious. To find it, we ask the client, "*Can you give me a couple of the situations or circumstances you're thinking about?*" Undoubtedly, they will, and you will then discover one or more new *business events* that weren't considered before. Add the new *business events* to your **Project Business Event List (Parking Lot)**, and then –working with your project subject-matter experts – develop the new **Business Process Diagrams** that support those *business events*.

3.7 How to Use Verb Context in the 'BRT Questions'

So far, I have said very little about how to select the verb construct to bind the two Objects in the 'BRT Question' together so you can have a context for the question. Let me remind you of how the 'BRT Questions' are structured:

QUESTION # 1:

Structure: "Could the {anchor OBJECT} {relationship context verb} just <u>one</u> {intersecting OBJECT}?"

Or, in plain English:

"Could the <u>SALESPERSON</u> serve just <u>one</u> <u>CUSTOMER</u>?" (Answer: *"Yes."*)

QUESTION # 2:

Structure: "Could the {anchor OBJECT} {relationship context verb} <u>several</u> {intersecting OBJECTs}?"

Or, in plain English:

"Could the <u>SALESPERSON</u> serve <u>several</u> <u>CUSTOMER</u>s?" (Answer: *"Yes."*)

QUESTION # 3:

Structure: "Might the {anchor OBJECT} never {relationship context verb} <u>any</u> {intersecting OBJECTs} at all?"

Or, in plain English:

"Might the <u>SALESPERSON</u> never serve <u>any</u> <u>CUSTOMER</u>s at all?" (Answer: *"Yes."*)

QUESTION # 4: "Under what circumstances might that be true?"
(Answer: *"They leave the company before they serve their first customer."*)

All of these questions are based on the **BUSINESS RULES TABLE** in Fig.3.29, with the answers written as 1, N, 0 under **CUSTOMER** and across from **SALESPERSON**.

So, how did we know to use the verb *'to serve'*? Lucky guess? How do we know what the verb construct should be for any 'BRT Question'?

BRT		Customer
1	Salesperson	1, N, 0
1	Customer	

Fig. 3.29: Partial Business Rules Table – Salesperson : Customer

The verb you choose to use is determined by the business process you are dealing with. For example, if the process you're working on has to do with the sale of products to customers, the **Business Process Diagram** (Fig. 3.30) will have a verb assigned to it that defines the process under which the data is related.

One way to find an appropriate verb to define the relationship between two Objects is to ask the clients or subject-matter experts who are present in your requirements *discovery* sessions. After all, they know their business.

However, if you do this I guarantee that you will get lots and lots of debate about what the right verb could be. If there are seven people in the room with you, you'll get eleven opinions on what's right and what's wrong. The reason for this is because you're asking them an open-ended question *("So, what verb might we use here?")*, which is designed for discussion rather than a direct answer. So, don't go there. You'll spin wheels 'til the cows come home.

It is far better that you select what you think is an appropriate verb (right or wrong) and go with

Fig. 3.30: Business Process Diagram – "Sell Product"

that. The important point is that the verb you chose must be contextual – that is, in the context of the business process – and must make sense in your 'BRT Questions'. The chosen verb will not necessarily be the one you used in the **Business Process Diagram**, like "**Sell Product**" in the process above (Fig. 3.30). But your chosen verb will reflect the context of that process. In the example we used earlier, based on this process, we used the verb "to serve" since this worked better in constructing the 'BRT Questions'.

But what about those situations when you have no idea what the right verb might be? What then? Out of all your verb choices in the language, you clearly can't just make one up without it making some kind of sense. So, what to do?

The answer, as with all good things, is with Shakespeare. The Bard had many good things to say, and arguably his most famous of all was The Question; which is precisely what we are discussing now – the 'BRT Question'. My friend Shakespeare wrote, *"To be or not to be … that is the question."*

To be.

But to use this effectively we have to start with the very first placeholder question. An example is below.

PLACEHOLDER QUESTION: "For a single, specific SALESPERSON how many CUSTOMERs might there be?" (Do not wait for an answer.)

We follow this immediately with the next three (and possibly four) 'BRT Questions'. However, to use the verb *'to be'* we have to slightly restructure the questions, as follows:

- 1st Question: **"Could there be just one CUSTOMER?"** (Answer: *"Yes."*)

- 2nd Question: **"Could there be several CUSTOMERs?"** (Answer: *"Yes."*)

- 3rd Question: **"Might there never be any CUSTOMERs at all?"** (Answer: *"Yes."*)

- 4th Question: **"Under what circumstances might that be true?"** (Answer: *"The salesperson leaves the company before they serve their first customer."*)

BRT		Customer
1	Salesperson	1, N, 0
1	Customer	

Fig. 3.31: Partial Business Rules Table – Salesperson : Customer

To make the questions work, the subject (**SALESPERSON**) is now mentioned in the placeholder question only, and it is implied in the subsequent questions. But it works, even though it can sometimes be awkward. I certainly wouldn't want to see a **Business Requirements Document** with the verb *'to be'* documented throughout all the Objects in the project. However, the purpose of this Shakespearean tactic is not to find the final verb, but to find a way of starting so your business partners and subject-matter experts can move ahead quickly. If necessary, you can change the verb construct later. This approach works extremely well; and has kept many discovery sessions rolling along without those awkward discussions when everyone in the room is arguing about what the right verb might be.

3.8 Opposite Cardinality in the Business Rules Table?

There is a commonly held misperception that opposite ends of a relationship between intersecting Objects must be the same. This is incorrect. Let me explain.

In the **Business Rules Table** in Fig. 3.32, the relationship cell **SALESPERSON-CUSTOMER** contains "NA", which means the client has decided that this relationship is 'not applicable' to their business requirements. There could be any number of reasons why they have no interest in this relationship. One possibility is that it's outside the scope of the project. In such a case, this relationship cell would produce no business rules that can contribute to the project.

BRT		Salesperson	Customer
1	Salesperson		NA
1	Customer	1, N, 0	

Fig. 3.32: Partial Business Rules Table – Salesperson : Customer

The opposite end of this relationship, **CUSTOMER-SALESPERSON**, contains **1, N, 0** which would produce a full set of rules, and may even identify a new *business event* in the reason for the "0" relationship.

BRT	Salesperson	Customer
1 Salesperson		NA
1 Customer	1, N, 0	

Fig. 3.33: Partial Business Rules Table –
Salesperson : Customer

It is definitely not true that the relationship between two Objects must be the same from both directions. Neither is it true that a relationship between two Objects will be different in the opposite direction.

Chapter 4. The Business Processes – How to Define Functionality

Contents

The business processes are arguably the most important part of the system requirements to your business partners and subject-matter experts. They think in terms of *what the system should do*, while the analyst must think in terms of what information the system must know about and have access to so it can support the business. That means we really have to focus on the Objects and the business rules. The Objects define the data we have to keep track of, and the business rules define the circumstances under which required data must exist. Your clients and subject-matter experts, however, will naturally want to focus on the processes required by the system, and what those processes should do.

Before exploring business processes we need to better understand the components that make up those processes, and we need to understand that a 'process model' can't stand on its own. The **Business Requirements Document** must consist of **all** required documentation, not just diagrams that describe the processes.

4.1 The Business Requirements Document

The **Business Requirements Document** is organized first by *business event* and secondly by Object, with each Object being defined only once.

You will recall that a *business event* is an essential condition, a circumstance, a situation, a state or an external requirement that the target business area must respond to or deal with in order to successfully support the organization's key business objectives, goals, or mission.

A *business event* also does not reflect ***how*** something is done; it represents ***what*** must be done without regard to a particular technology or a particular way of doing things.

You will recall that *business events* come in four flavors:

Situation Event – non-controlled

"The Customer Buys a Product"
"The Product Shipment Arrives from a Supplier"
"The Customer has Exceeded Their Credit Limit"

External Event – based on third party need

"The Government Requires Notification of Employee Earnings"
"The Customer Requests a Higher Credit Limit"

Temporal Event – based on time

"The Customer's Credit Card Expires"
"It is Time to Pay the Supplier"
"It is Time to Increase the Customer's Credit Limit"

Internal Event – based on a decision

"The Company Decides to Cancel the Customer's Credit Card"
"The Company Decides to Issue a Loan to the Customer"

Also, *business events* <u>never</u> start with a verb. That's because a *business event* is <u>not</u> a process. A *business event* is a <u>condition</u>, <u>circumstance</u>, <u>state</u> or <u>external requirement</u> that must be supported by a process. The process that supports a *business event* is illustrated by, preferably, a **Business Process Diagram**, which is similar to (looks like) but not the same as a data flow diagram.

Data flow diagrams are discussed extensively in Tom DeMarco's delightful original work, ***Structured Analysis and System Specification***. Scores of other books have been published since then, with almost all of them based on his earlier work. DeMarco's is still the easiest to read and understand. However, while the **Business Process Diagram** looks very much like a data flow diagram, it is limited to one process only, rather than several. This, too, goes to the idea that we should "partition the effort to minimize complexity" and therefore be more "agile" in approaching business requirements.

What we do to deal with a *business event* is documented in the **Business Requirements Document** with the content described on the next page. The documentation in the **Business Requirements Document** is organized by *business event* first and by Object second.

Some of my colleagues insist that both <u>data models</u> and <u>process models</u> are necessary for a complete requirements specification. I respectfully disagree with that approach. That's very old-school, and takes a lot of unnecessary time. Data models – for which I use the Chen-type of **Object-Relationship Diagram** in this book – represent essentially a database view. Our business partners and clients really have no interest in the database view. Their primary interest is in business functionality, and appropriate deployment of technology to support their business needs. However, in addition to business behavioral rules, the accesses to data that are required by the target business area are illustrated in the **Business Rules Tables** that support each process. While this is mostly transparent to your business partners, database analysts and designers should recognize **Business Rules Tables** as prescriptions for database access based on the requirements of the business.

The Business Requirements Document

Project Business Event List
(from the *Project Scope Blitz*)

- List of project *business events* from the *Project Scope Blitz*, including business area ownership and involvement, and requirement priority.

SALES AND PROCUREMENT PROJECT
AIR Telecom Inc.

	List of Potential Events	SALES	MARKETING	PURCHASING	ACCOUNTING	Priority (1, 2, 3)
1	A Customer Buys a Product	★	★		★	1
2	A Customer Requests an Unavailable Product	★	★			1
3	A Product is Returned by a Customer	★	★		★	1
4	It is Time to Determine a Salesperson's Commissions	★			★	2
5	It is Time to Order a Product from a Supplier	★	★	★	★	1
6	It is Time to Pay a Supplier for Product Delivered	★	★	★	★	1

Total Number of Events –	6
Pilot & Copilot: Days to BRD –	2.7
Pilot Only: Days to BRD –	4.4

Fig. 4.1: A Short Business Event List for a Project

For each Event (*n* occurrences)

- A **Business Process Diagram** that supports the *business event*.
- A task-based narrative for the Business process.
- References or links to Object definitions.
- A list of Business Areas affected by the Business process
- A Business Rules Table for Objects supporting the business process.
- Any Implementation (design solution) considerations.

For each Object (*n* occurrences)

- Definition of the Object.
- Business Rules for the Object.
- Data attributes for the Object.
- Primary (unique) identifier.

The Business Rules Table (BRT)

- Matrix of intersecting Objects.
- Cardinality (0,1,N) for each Object.

BRT	customer	product	payment
1 customer		1,N,0	1,N,0
1 product	1,N,0		1,N,0
1 payment	1	1,N	

Fig. 4.2: Example of a Business Rules Table

Business Process Diagram symbols

Business Process Diagram.

The **Business Process Diagram** illustrates the required tasks and planned responses of the target business area to a specific *business event*. Each **Business Process Diagram** must have a written narrative to describe the process. This narrative supports the diagram so readers of the documentation can understand the business requirements. The diagram must have definitions of all the participating Objects, their data attributes, and business rules. A single **Business Process Diagram** can support more than one *business event*.

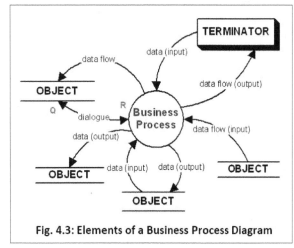

Fig. 4.3: Elements of a Business Process Diagram

Fig. 4.3 is an illustration of the elements of a **Business Process Diagram**, and Fig. 4.4 is a diagram specific to the *business event* "**The Customer Buys a Product**".

While a picture is worth a thousand words, this diagram is not sufficient to describe business requirements: It needs a brief narrative, Object definitions, data attributes and business rules before it is complete.

Fig. 4.4: Business Process Diagram – ``Sell Product``

Terminator.

A Terminator is a source of information or destination for information from a process. A Terminator, which may be inside or outside your organization, is not directly under the control of the business process which receives it or sends information to it. A Terminator has its own set of processes and data, but these are outside the domain of the process that interfaces with it. *Use Case* practitioners might call a Terminator an "Actor", but that's only part of the story. It is definitely not a **Primary Actor** (one who does something in the system, since that implies a "how" or a technology, since there are three kinds of technologies: Software, hardware and peopleware). However, a Terminator can be either or both a **Secondary Actor** (provides a service or data) and an **Offstage Actor** (has an interest in the system, and receives data). A Terminator is simply a source or a destination of information. Some, but not all Terminators are also Objects in our business processes; but only if we need to remember something about the Terminator, or need to look it up (among several) so information can be sent to it.

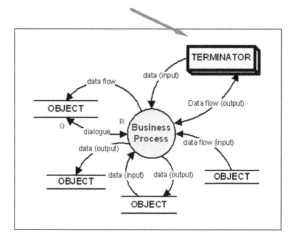

Fig. 4.5: Business Process Diagram (The Terminator)

Object.

An Object is a repository of data shown in **Business Process Diagrams**.

- An Object is a repository of logically grouped non-redundant data.

- An Object in a **Business Process Diagram** is exactly the same as an Object in an **Object-Relationship Diagram** (an Object by any other name is still an Object; the shape of it doesn't matter), but is a different shape because the IT industry established these standards many years ago, when the two sides (data and process) weren't really seeing eye-to-eye.

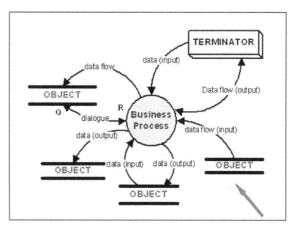

Fig. 4.6: Business Process Diagram (The Object)

- An Object in a **Business Process Diagram** contains all the data items attributed to the Object, in accordance with **The 5 Rules of Business Data** (see section 2.4).

- An Object in a **Business Process Diagram** contains all the business rules attributed to it from the **Business Rules Table** specific to that **Business Process Diagram** (see Chapter 3: The Business Rules Table).

Process Narrative.

A task-based process narrative must be written for each **Business Process Diagram** in plain language. It must specify clearly what is to be done with each data flow and describes the planned response to support the business process. It can be written in either of two styles: point form or structured narrative.

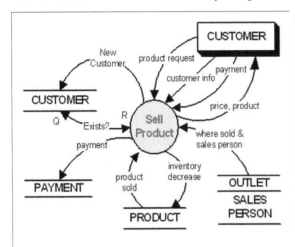

Fig. 4.7: Business Process Diagram – with 2 narrative styles

Point Form Style

For each request for a product from the customer:

- Find out if the **CUSTOMER** exists in our system.
- Find the **PRODUCT** sold.
- If it is available, give it to the **CUSTOMER** with the price.
- Accept the **PAYMENT** from the **CUSTOMER**.
- Remember the **PAYMENT**.
- Remember the **SALESPERSON** who served the **CUSTOMER**, and in which **OUTLET**.
- Reduce inventory by the quantity of **PRODUCT** sold.
- If it is a new **CUSTOMER**, get the **CUSTOMER** information from the customer.
- Remember the new **CUSTOMER** information.

Fig. 4.8: Task-based Narrative – Point Form Style

Structured Narrative Style

For each request for a product from the customer, find the **PRODUCT**. If it is available give it to the **CUSTOMER** with the cost. Accept the **PAYMENT** from the **CUSTOMER**. Remember the **PAYMENT** and the sales transaction, including the **SALESPERSON** who served the **CUSTOMER**, and in which **OUTLET**. Reduce inventory by the quantity of the **PRODUCT** sold. If it is a new customer, remember the **CUSTOMER**.

Fig. 4.9: Task-based Narrative – Structured Narrative Style

Data flow.

A *data flow* represents the directional movement of information between a process and an Object or Terminator. A data flow must always be labeled for its contents when the data flow is between a process and a Terminator. However, it does not have to be labeled if it is between the process and an Object. This is because an Object is about one thing, and one thing only. While a data flow may only contain some of the data in

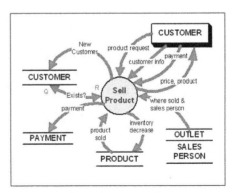

Fig. 4.10: Business Process Diagram – illustrating data flows (bold lines)

an Object, the Object itself is not mystery data. An Object is *something* specific. It is helpful, however, to always label a data flow since this makes it clear what is "riding" the data flow. You don't have to use data item names. Label it any way you like, as long as the label communicates effectively what the data flow is all about. This means the reader has to understand it, not just the writer.

Dialogue Data flow.

A dialogue data flow is a data flow with arrows at each end showing the "dialogue" between a process and (a) an Object that contains data, or (b) a Terminator. For example, to query the **CUSTOMER** Object we can put the query "*exists*?" on the data flow, and a "**Q**" (for query) and "**R**" (for response) on each end of the data flow to illustrate that there is a dialogue.

Strict use of data item names on a data flow is not required, although this was the convention in the past. You can put anything you like on the data flow if it helps you to communicate better. If an Object is well named and properly attributed with data, without redundancy, then it will not be a mystery to know what

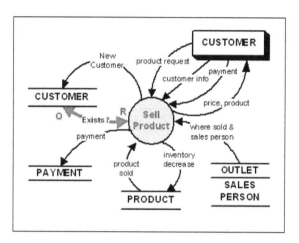

Fig. 4.11: Business Process Diagram – illustrating data flows (bold lines)

data the Object consists of. One thing for sure: An Object will not be a variety-show data store containing all kinds of information about all kinds of things. Because Objects are limited it enables you to use data flows better, even putting verbs on them.

Stacked Objects.

Diagrams can sometimes get pretty busy, especially if there are a lot of participating Objects. So, we sometimes stack Objects to conserve space, as you see in Fig. 4.12. But we can't stack all the Objects, making one big stack, which would not be helpful in understanding the diagram. Objects should only be stacked if they are related to the subject of the data flows – such as the example in Fig. 4.12.

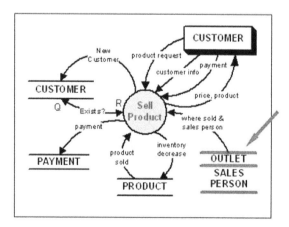

Fig. 4.12: Business Process Diagram – illustrating related stacked Objects

4.2 Finding the Business Requirements – 6 Steps

Each *business event* or circumstance encountered by the business must be handled by the business in a prescribed manner; i.e., with a planned response. This means the circumstance or condition the business encounters must first be recognized as part of a process; i.e., there must be a stimulus that identifies the existence of the *business event*.

> A *"business event"* is an *essential* business condition, situation, circumstance, state or external requirement which the affected business area must respond to or deal with in order to carry on operations to successfully support its key business objectives.

The stimulus that tells us what circumstance the business has encountered – what the *business event* is – can be either temporal (like a date or a specific day), or it can be a specific value of data, such as a **CUSTOMER** exceeding their *credit limit*. Time can also be represented by data, such as a *due date*.

> - **The customer buys a product**
> - **It is time to order a product from a supplier**
> - **The product arrives from a supplier**
> - **It is time to pay a supplier**

The stimulus, regardless of the form it takes, identifies the *business event*. For example, "It is Time to Pay a Supplier" is a condition that exists *at a specific time*. Usually it's the *due date*, which would be the stimulus that identifies the existence of the *business event*. This is part of a process that supports the *business event* "It is Time to Pay a Supplier".

Once the stimulus has been identified we have to determine what should be done with the information. For example, if we know that the *due date* tells us that "**It is Time to Pay a Supplier**", the question becomes "what do we want to do about it?" After shaping the process with the client – i.e., finding out *what we want to do about it* – then we ask the question, "and what do we want to record or remember about this?"

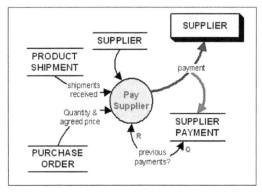

Fig. 4.13: Business Process Diagram – ``Pay Supplier``, showing planned response, with narrative

In the example in Fig. 4.13, we pay the supplier (this is *what we do about it*), and we record the payment (this is *what we remember about it*).

- Periodically, find those shipments received from suppliers that have not been completely paid.
- Determine the amount owed based on the amount of product received and the agreed price.
- Deduct any previous payments against the same purchase order.
- Pay the supplier, and remember the payment.

In essence, we asked just three basic questions, which enabled us to build the **Business Process Diagram** in Fig. 4.13.

1. "How do I know that "It is Time to Pay a Supplier"**?** (The answer identifies the stimulus.)

2. "What do I want to do about it?" (The answer tells us about the process itself.)

3. "What do I want to remember or record about what I've done?" (The answer tells us what we will record, and therefore look up at some other time.)

The 6 Steps to a Business Requirements Document

There are six basic steps to follow to complete the **<u>Business Requirements Document</u>**.

1. Conduct Project Scope Blitz.
2. Plan the Project's Discovery Sessions.
3. Develop a Business Process.
4. Identify Business Objects.
5. Query a Business Rules Table
6. Issue the Business Requirements Document

STEP 1. Conduct Project Scope Blitz: This is the starting point for all projects. Convene a ½-day or 1-day *Project Scope Blitz*, as an interactive discovery session with the project's sponsors, clients, subject-matter experts, other key people and interested senior persons.

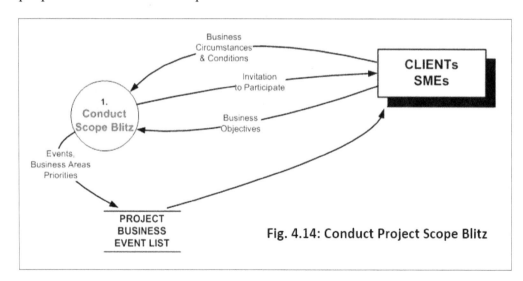

Fig. 4.14: Conduct Project Scope Blitz

The Process:

- Determine the best time to conduct a *Project Scope Blitz*.

- Issue a <u>Scope Blitz Discovery Invitation</u> to all clients and prospective subject-matter experts.

- At the scheduled time, conduct the *Project Scope Blitz* with clients and subject-matter experts.

- During the *Project Scope Blitz* with clients and SMEs, determine *business event* that are in-scope (as many as possible, but apply the 80/20 Rule, since other *business events* will be found during the detailed discovery sessions).

> - The customer buys a product
> - It is time to order a product from a supplier
> - The product arrives from a supplier
> - It is time to pay a supplier

Fig. 4.15: Partial Event List

- Record *business events* that are mentioned but are out-of-scope.

- Issue the **PROJECT BUSINESS EVENT LIST** to all participants as soon as practical after the *Project Scope Blitz*.

STEP 2. Plan Discovery Sessions: After finishing the ½-day or 1-day Project Scope Blitz, and a short (or long) list of *business events* has been produced, it's time to plan the detailed client-interactive discovery sessions for the project.

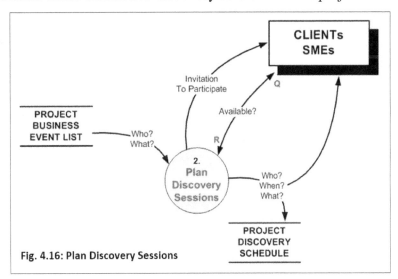

Fig. 4.16: Plan Discovery Sessions

The Process:

- Based on the **PROJECT BUSINESS EVENT LIST** produced from the *Project Scope Blitz*, determine the availability of clients and subject-matter experts to participate in detailed client-interactive discovery sessions for the project.

- Create a **PROJECT DISCOVERY SCHEDULE**, with participants and dates, for each *business event* on the **PROJECT BUSINESS EVENT LIST**.

- When the schedule is complete, issue the **PROJECT DISCOVERY SCHEDULE** and a formal "Invitation to Participate" in the discovery sessions to affected clients and SMEs.

STEP 3. Develop a Business Process <u>and</u>

STEP 4. Identify Business Objects.

Developing a business process and identifying the Objects that support that business process must be done together, at the same time. These are not, and cannot be, separate activities. Data and process are completely integrated – they have a symbiotic relationship – just like verbs and nouns are used together to make a sentence. Also, data attribution at the high level (i.e., finding a home for those data items that are needed) is done while defining the business process. Other, detailed data items can be attributed to Objects outside these discovery sessions.

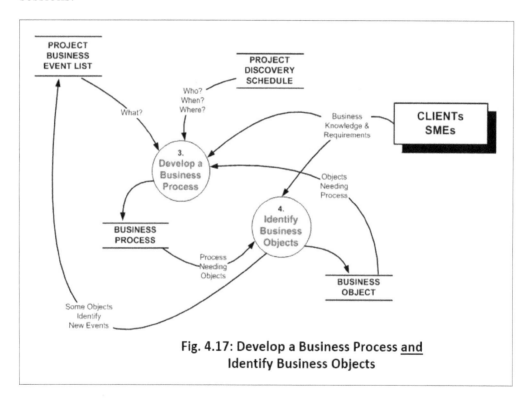

Fig. 4.17: Develop a Business Process <u>and</u>
Identify Business Objects

The Process:

- Periodically, based on the **PROJECT DISCOVERY SCHEDULE**, meet with subject-matter experts to develop business requirements for the business.
- For each *business event* on the **PROJECT BUSINESS EVENT LIST**, develop the supporting **BUSINESS PROCESS**, based on discovery dialogue with project subject-matter experts.
- By dialogue with business subject-matter experts, determine the **BUSINESS OBJECT**s that are required to support the **BUSINESS PROCESS**.

- At a high level (apply the 80/20 Rule), attribute data to **BUSINESS OBJECT**s according to <u>The 5 Rules of Business Data</u> (see section 2.4).

- For those Objects and data items that identify the need for additional *business events*, add those *business events* to the **PROJECT BUSINESS EVENT LIST**.

- For those Objects that identify the need for additional **BUSINESS PROCESS**es, develop those additional **BUSINESS PROCESS**es.

STEP 5. Query a Business Rules Table: After completing a **Business Process Diagram**, create a **Business Rules Table** for the diagram, populated with the Objects that are part of the **Business Process Diagram**.

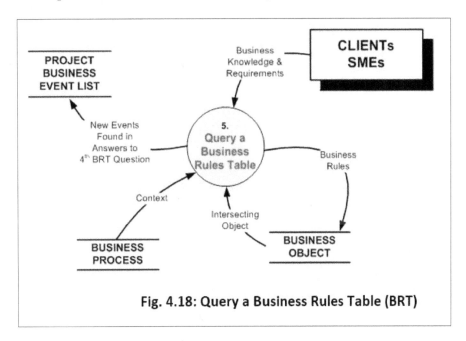

Fig. 4.18: Query a Business Rules Table (BRT)

<u>**The Process:**</u>

NOTE: This is not a discrete process. Querying the **Business Rules Table** is done immediately after each **Business Process Diagram** is finished.

- For two intersecting **BUSINESS OBJECT**s specific to a **BUSINESS PROCESS**, determine the <u>Business Rules</u> in the context of the **BUSINESS PROCESS**, by asking the <u>BRT Questions</u>.

- For each <u>Business Rule</u> determined, attribute the Rule to the **BUSINESS OBJECT** that forms the anchor (subject) of the <u>BRT Question</u>.

- In the **Business Rules Table**, annotate the <u>Rules</u> (1,N and/or 0) in the intersection cell of the two queried **BUSINESS OBJECT**s.

- Write each <u>Business Rule</u> in plain language under the **BUSINESS OBJECT** to which the <u>Rule</u> has been attributed.

STEP 6. Issue the Business Requirements Document: After completing **Business Process Diagrams** for all the *business events* on the <u>**PROJECT BUSINESS EVENT LIST**</u>, including the ones found during the detailed discovery sessions with clients and subject-matter experts, all the documentation is organized as part of the <u>**BUSINESS REQUIREMENTS DOCUMENT**</u>. This document is then issued to those who need it.

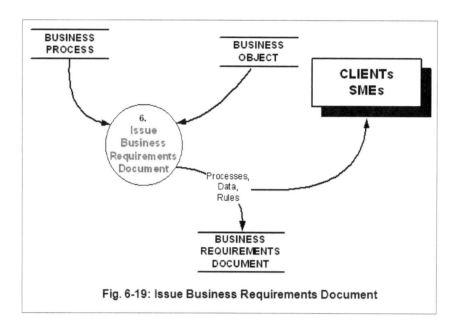

Fig. 6-19: Issue Business Requirements Document

<u>**The Process:**</u>

- For each <u>**BUSINESS PROCESS**</u> that has been completely defined, record it as part of the <u>**BUSINESS REQUIREMENTS DOCUMENT**</u>.

- When done, issue the <u>**BUSINESS REQUIREMENTS DOCUMENT**</u> to clients and subject-matter experts, as required.

We will discuss different and more agile ways of organizing the documentation and distributing it later in the text. The traditional way of documenting, distributing and getting sign-offs is quite contrary to how an agile organization can operate.

4.3 The Anatomy of a Business Requirement

The example we have selected to go through in considerable detail is a (partial) personal *accounts payable* system. We all have one of these, whether we use software to manage paying our bills or we manage it directly out of our checkbook. Since it is intended as an example of how to go through the 6 Steps to create a business requirements specification, we are not going to go down every possible road in terms of variable answers to questions or other such considerations. It's an example, and much in real life can be different.

Parsing the Business Processes

The first step is to conduct a *Project Scope Blitz* to produce a short (or long) list of *business events* – conditions, circumstances, situations and other external requirements – that the target business area must include in its scope. One of the objectives of the initial *Project Scope Blitz* is to get together with all the senior project people – the sponsors, the key stakeholders, the business and subject-matter experts – and outline how the work will progress, what it will look like and how long it will take. In other words, to manage expectations. Part of managing expectations is to get a real handle on the project's scope, and to have the agreement of the key people involved. The way to accomplish this, we have found, is to create a list of in-scope *business events*. (There's more involved in a *Project Scope Blitz*, but we'll get to that later.)

We can get initial *business events* from the business and subject-matter experts by leading an interactive session that searches out the desired *business events* for the project. This presumes that your business experts know their business and they have a pretty good idea of what they need to support their business needs – not the technology application, but the business functionality.[1]

You certainly don't have to find all the *business events* that might make up your project. That would be difficult, at best. All you need is a few entries on a short list to get you started. If you have just a few *business events*, then you will be able to find all the others through answers to your 'BRT Questions', and specifically the fourth question – "under what circumstances would that be true?"[2]

In this example we'll limit ourselves to starting with just two *business events*. However, we expect to find other *business events* through the 'BRT Questions', and if we do (and they are in scope) we'll add them to our **Project Business Event List (Parking Lot)**[3] so we can work on them later.

---

[1] Your clients do know their business. With well-structured and focused questions we will get very precise answers from them.

[2] See Chapter 3, The Business Rules Table – How to Find the Questions to Ask.

[3] The **Project Business Event List** is the list of *business events* first produced from the interactive *Project Scope Blitz*. During the detailed discovery sessions with subject-matter experts, several new *business events* are usually discovered (*business events* that were not on the original list, and some that were not even thought to be part of the project). These are usually found in answers to the fourth 'BRT Question', although some are also found when the Object and Data Inclusion and Exclusion Questions are asked. As new in-scope *business events* are discovered, they are added to the **Project Business Event List (Parking Lot)**, and we can return to them when it's time to do so. In this way, progress is also very visible to clients, and there is no "*trust me, we'll deal with it later*".

In our example we won't actually work through the newly discovered *events*, but we will add them to our list, so you can see how quite a few new *events* can be found through the 'BRT Questions'.

The two *business events* we will work through are ➔

Project Business Event List
- A Bill Arrives from a Supplier
- It is Time to Pay a Supplier

The first *business event* is, "**A Bill Arrives from a Supplier**".

Fig. 4.20: Initial Project Event List

Business Process Diagrams

The first question we ask is, *"How do I know that ... (insert event statement here). For example, for our *business event* "**A Bill Arrives from a Supplier**" the question would be *"How do I know that a bill arrives from a supplier?"*

In this case the answer could be, "*We know the bill arrived from the supplier because we received it in the mail.*"

The "mail" can, of course, mean many things. It could mean the bill arrived in the mailbox attached to your house or apartment, or it could be the mailbox in your computer. If we specify either of these "physical" options at this stage in the project, then we are biasing the solution design, or at the very least we are limiting ourselves to our current way of thinking. This would make it all the more difficult to discover re-engineering opportunities when we look at the potential design solutions later.

Instead, we look for the basic concept behind "mail" and the *net flow of data*. What this means is … we look for the source of the data, rather than the physical handler, such as an email system or postal delivery. In our earlier definition of a Terminator we said, "*It is a source of input…*" from outside the system. In this example we get the bill from a supplier. We illustrate this by using **Business Process Diagram** symbols, showing the process as a bubble, and the data we received from the supplier as a data flow with an arrow from the supplier as input to the process in our system.[4]

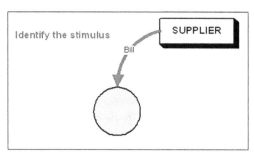

Fig. 4.21: Business Process "stimulus"

---

[4] Note that a stimulus that identifies a *business event* and initiates a process does not always come from a Terminator. A stimulus can also be time, or data that's part of an Object.

The second question is, *"What are we going to do about it?"* In our accounts payable example it means we have to determine what we're going to do with the bill after we receive it. While the immediate response might simply be, *"pay it,"* that's covered by our second *business event*, "**It is Time to Pay a Supplier**".

(At all times, we must stay focused on the current *business event* to the exclusion of all others. In other words, **Business Process Diagrams** are joined by data, through Objects, and never through the flow of data. By trying to join various processes by way of data flows, rather than data items that make up Objects, we would end up with meta-*business events* that include everything, such as "**A Bill Arrives from a Supplier**" <u>and</u> "**It is Time to Pay a Supplier**". If you end up doing a whole lot of things that are lumped together this way, you're probably violating our First Principle, "partition the effort to minimize complexity".) **5**

Returning to what we're going to do with the bill we receive from the supplier (such as a phone bill), the question was *"What are we going to do about it?"*

Our project subject-matter expert has informed us, *"We only accept bills from recognized and approved suppliers."* With that information we can add two data flows to our **Business Process Diagram**, as shown on the right. Each data flow represents a task.

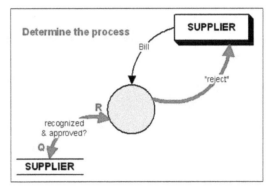

Fig. 4.22: Business Process "tasks"

In a real business system we would, of course, check the bill against a purchase order to determine its legitimacy. However, our example (minimized to reduce complexity) is a personal accounts payable system.

The last question to our subject-matter expert (SME) is, *"What do we need to record or remember about this process?"* In our example this means – now that we have received a bill and checked that it's from a recognized supplier – that we want to record the bill received from the supplier. We can draw this as illustrated in our model below.

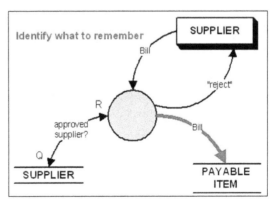

Fig. 4.23: Business Process "remembering data"

5 Remember the First Principle of Analysis – Simplicity: "Partition the effort to minimize complexity." This means breaking it down into small pieces so we can focus on one manageable piece at a time.

Before we go on to the next part, let's review how to determine the direction of the arrow on a diagram. Data flows (and their arrowheads) can only go in two directions – in or out of the process (the bubble). The data flow either goes out of the process or it comes into the process.

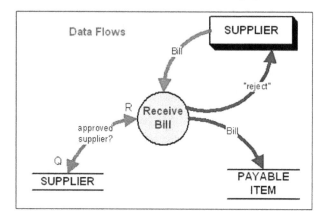

Fig. 4.24: Direction of data flows

When a data flow comes into the process (the bubble) it means we are retrieving data from an Object or we have received data from a Terminator.

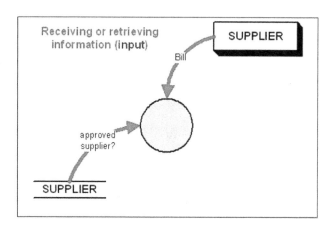

Fig. 4.25: Data flows coming into a process

When a data flow goes out of a process, it means we are recording data in an Object or we are sending some form of data to a Terminator (i.e., to a destination outside the system or business unit's immediate processes).

Fig. 4.26: Data flows going out of a process

When there is a dialogue data flow there are arrowheads on each end of the data flow. This represents two separate data flows – one to find the right record or data, and another to return the data – for the same subject data. By drawing a single data flow in this manner, we're just conserving space, and we're illustrating that something specific is directly related; i.e., two ends of the same thing. The **'Q'** represents "query", and the **'R'** represents "response". In the example in Fig. 4.27

Fig. 4.27: Dialogue Data Flow

we could read it as, *"Find the record of an approved supplier that matches the query. If the query finds that the supplier is on record and approved, tell me. If not, tell me that too."*

This now leaves us with a complete diagram for the *business event* **"A Bill Arrives from a Supplier"** (as shown on the right, Fig. 4.28). But lots of things haven't been done yet: We haven't given a name to the process and labeled it; nor have we written a narrative to describe it. We also haven't done any data discovery and attribution; and we haven't completed the **Business**

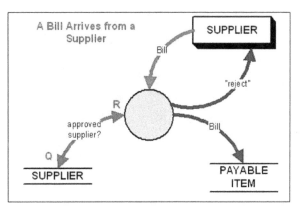

Fig. 4.28: Business Process to support the Business Event "A Bill Arrives from a Supplier"

Rules Table to find and document the business rules for Objects that support this particular circumstance ("**A Bill Arrives from a Supplier**").

Some of these things are done in parallel with the drawing of the **Business Process Diagram** to support a *business event*. This is particularly true for how we go about discovering Objects and how we go about attributing data items that we find. Creating the **Business Rules Table**, asking the 'BRT Questions', and generating the business rules is the very last thing that's done after the diagram has been completed, including writing the descriptive narrative and attributing data to the Objects.

You will recall that the very first question we asked our subject-matter experts was, *"How do I know that a bill arrives from a supplier?"* This resulted in finding the stimulus (bill arrives from supplier), which led to the partial diagram on the right.

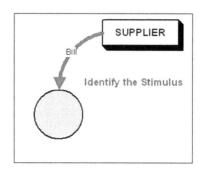

Fig. 4.29: Business Process with "stimulus" identified

As the subject-matter experts answer the next question *("What are we going to do about it?")*, your SMEs could respond with an answer that might be at the highest level of abstraction or at the lowest level of detail. As an analyst, it is your responsibility to decipher what they have said and to determine what's a data item and what's an Object.

Because we now have to find the data that supports the process, we usually supplement the original question with another: *"What do we need to know about or remember about this process?"* For each noun, you must determine if it consists of *two or more component parts*. If it does, it's a noun "with substance" and it complies with Business Data Rule # 3 (see Chapter 2: The Business Object). That's an Object. If the noun does not consist of more than one data item, then it's just another data item for which you have to find a home.

Another way of initially identifying Objects that are needed to support a *business event* situation – and perhaps the best way to start – is to use the nouns you find in the *business event* statement itself. For example, in the *business event* "**A Bill Arrives from a Supplier**" there are two nouns – bill and supplier. Are these nouns "of substance"? Can we imagine each of them consisting of two or more data items? Sure ... we can imagine the Object **BILL** consisting of data such as *due date* and *amount due*. The other Object, **SUPPLIER**, could include data items such as *supplier name*, *supplier address*, *contact name* and *phone number*.

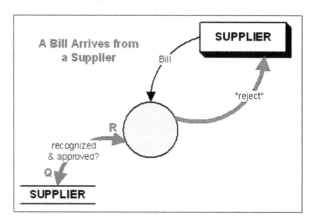

Fig. 4.30: Business Process with SUPPLIER Object

Since **SUPPLIER** is clearly an Object (see below), then we must ask our subject-matter experts if they want a record of authorized suppliers. If the answer is *"yes,"* then we have an Object that we must document – and we can immediately attribute some of the data we uncovered.

SUPPLIER
- supplier name
- supplier address
- contact name
- phone #

Fig. 4.31: SUPPLIER data attributes

For **BILL** we must ask our subject-matter experts if we want to remember (or record) the *due date* and *amount due*. If the answer is *"yes,"* then this is also an Object that we must include, and we can immediately attribute the data we uncovered.

These questions should all stimulate other questions. We might even find the subject-matter experts want to call the bill a **PAYABLE ITEM**, and want to include some other data attributes (which we won't include here, so we can keep the example small).

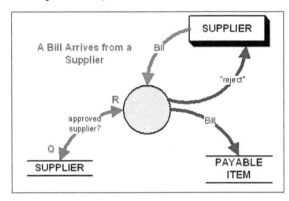

Fig. 4.32: Business Process with
PAYABLE ITEM Object

PAYABLE ITEM
• Due date
• Amount due

Fig. 4.33: PAYABLE ITEM
data attributes

Discussions with clients and subject-matter experts will tend to bring out the remaining Objects and the data that make up the Objects. In this particular example, there are no more Objects needed to support the *business event* **"A Bill Arrives from a Supplier"**.

How do we know that we have put the data attributes with the right Objects? Business Data Rule # 1 (see Chapter 2: The Business Object) states, *"Attribute the data item to the Object it describes best, and to no other Object."* It appears that *due date* and *amount due* describe **PAYABLE ITEM** best, while *supplier name*, *supplier address*, *contact name* and *phone #* best describe **SUPPLIER**.

The next step is to write a plain yet descriptive narrative. The narrative has to be clear, concise, unambiguous, in plain business language – and brief.

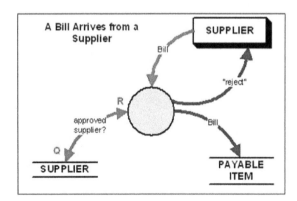

Fig. 4.34: Business Process supports the
business event "A Bill Arrives from a Supplier"

You will notice that at this time we have left the bubble that denotes the process unlabeled – blank and unnamed. That's intentional, and we're going to leave it unnamed until we have written the descriptive narrative necessary to support the diagram.

Our objective is to write a narrative that clearly explains the **Business Process Diagram** in as much detail as necessary, but no more. Our narrative must be in plain language – easily understood by our business partners – without any technobabble. We must stay away from writing great prose or even a novel. All of these are unnatural to our business partners. The end result must be a narrative that's easily understood by the business partners and the technical team[6].

So, where do you start? To help with the structure of the sentences, we have identified a few key words that will help you develop a usable narrative that's understandable to all. These five key words can be used to build just about any narrative:

1. "For each …"
2. "Periodically …"
3. "Determine …"
4. "Remember (or record) …"
5. "Find (or identify) …"

But how do we know exactly how many narrative statements are needed for any given business process? Is it simply stream-of-consciousness? Is it roaming around the china shop of words until we figure out what the text should be, based on brute thinking force? Does it require a major in English? Does it involve smoke and mirrors? Or will just plain magic do the trick?

Well, there is a way. Let me tell you about it.

---

[6] The <u>system</u> specification narrative has been debated for many years now. As incredible as it may seem, there are many who still teach how to write "Structured English" or (sigh) "Tight English", vintage when wheels were square. We're now well into the 21st century and there are many who are still teaching the methods and tools of the 1960s and 1970s. There is a new "Structured Narrative" that is much better suited to today's world. There is also a clear difference between a technical <u>system</u> specification and a <u>business</u> requirements specification. The descriptive narratives in this book are intended for use with business requirements and not for technical system specifications.

We determine the narrative needed by identifying an implicit task[7] for each data flow that comes into or goes out of the process. Visually, it looks like the illustration on the right (Fig. 4.35); although we don't draw those little nodes on our real diagrams, we just write the descriptive narratives.

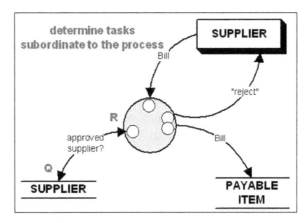

Fig. 4.35: Business Process with "task nodes" illustrated

Each of these nodes must have an explanatory narrative; or, better put, each node must be referenced in some way in the descriptive narrative that you write. You can use at least two different styles when producing your narrative, the Structured Narrative Style, or the Point Form Style. You can also develop your own style, as long as your narrative text refers to each of the data flows entering or leaving the process. You may have to add additional text to describe the transformation of data, such as calculations or other formulas.

For the **Business Process Diagram** below (which supports the *business event* "**A Bill Arrives from a Supplier**"), you could produce a narrative similar to either of the styles below the diagram.

Fig. 4.36: Business Process with 2 types of descriptive narratives based on task nodes

Structured Narrative Style	**Point Form Style**
For each **bill** received, determine if it is from a recognized and approved **supplier**. If it is, remember it. If the **supplier** is not recognized, reject the **bill**.	1. Receive the **bill**. 2. Determine if it is from a recognized and approved **supplier**. 3. If it is, record it. 4. If the **supplier** is not recognized, reject the **bill**.

---

[7] A 'task' is an activity that is subordinate to a 'process'. A process consists of several tasks.

This form of *functional decomposition*[8], which is really process decomposition, is relatively straightforward. It enables you to quickly determine the tasks that make up a process.

Before we go on with our next *business event* in our accounts payable example, let's look at another example of process decomposition that enables us to easily write the narrative for the process.

For the diagram below, our objective is to pay the supplier for products received. Previous payments may already have been made (or not). After process decomposition to identify the subordinate tasks, we could have a task list, and narrative, as follows:

Point Form Style

1. Find **product shipment**s not completely paid.
2. Determine the amount owed, based on the amount of **product** received and the agreed price.
3. Deduct any previous **payment**s made against the same **purchase order**.
4. Find the **supplier**'s location and preferred method of payment.
5. Pay the **supplier**.
6. Record the **payment**.

Fig. 4.37: Business Process with 2 types of descriptive narratives based on task nodes

Structured Narrative Style

Periodically, find those **shipment**s received from **supplier**s that have not been completely paid. Determine the amount owed based on the amount of **product** received and the agreed price. Deduct any previous **payment**s against the same **purchase order**. Pay the **supplier**, and remember the **payment**.

---

[8] Originally, *functional decomposition* was used to divide engineering systems into segments such that each block on a block diagram could be described without an "and" or "or" in the description. Similarly, if you use the Point Form Style of narrative, each task that supports a process should stand alone and not link with other tasks using "and" or "or" in the descriptive text. However, pragmatism will suggest that you could often use one simple "and" statement (e.g., "Receive the video request and payment from the customer,") rather than the two separate statements, "Receive the video request from the customer" and "Receive the payment from the customer". But, since we're all wired a little different, you can choose any style you like, as long as it helps you communicate.

Once again, you can write itemized tasks (Point Form Style), or you can write simple sentences (Structured Narrative Style), as shown in Fig, 4.37.

The *business event* in this case is "**It is Time to Pay a Supplier**". If a *business event* starts with "**It is Time to ...**" we can often start the narrative with *"Periodically ..."* The writing style you chose to use is the one you are most comfortable with.

The new element we introduced into this diagram, in Fig. 4.37, is what is called a *split* or *divergent data* flow. In the example diagram on the right (Fig. 4.38), it means you are sending the payment to two places: the physical payment goes to the supplier (which could be a check or an electronic funds transfer); and the payment data is recorded so we can keep track of the supplier payment. While these two data flows that diverge represent the same thing (payment information), they will certainly be physically different in the implemented system.

Fig. 4.38: Business Process with "split" or "divergent"

In this example, relationships between Objects are absolutely necessary[9]. If the Objects are not somehow joined, we would not be able to find what we need. For example, we need to find the **SUPPLIER** record for a specific **PURCHASE ORDER**. We also need to find all the **SUPPLIER PAYMENT** records for a specific **PURCHASE ORDER**. These relationships necessitate *foreign keys* to join the Objects that need to be joined. (For a review of *Pointers to Related Objects*, see Chapter 2: The Business Object.) For us to create a business requirements specification that also consists of a prescription for the database design – but transparent to the client and the SMEs – we need to define which Objects must be joined to which other Objects under

Fig. 4.39: Business Process – Objects must be joined so they can be relational

---

[9] This is because Objects such as SUPPLIER only contain information about that specific Object, and not about any other Objects (such as payments from the supplier). It's all based on the 5 Rules of Business Data, particularly Rule # 1, "Attribute the data item to the Object it describes best, and to no other Object."

different circumstances (*business events*). We will do this through the **Business Rules Table**.[10]

We now have a complete diagram and narrative for the *business event* "**A Bill Arrives from a Supplier**". We have also identified the Objects and data items we need to support the process.

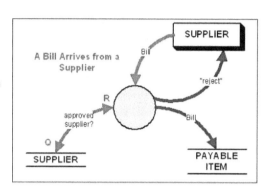

Fig. 4.40: Complete but unnamed Business Process

But we haven't named the process yet, which is the last thing we do before we build out the **Business Rules Table**.

We didn't name the process earlier (as you wanted to do) because that would have created an unconscious bias to make the narrative fit the name of the process. We have found that one of the best ways of freeing our mind from any predetermined path, or bias, is to name the process last, after the narrative is written.

Naming a process is a lot easier than it appears. The first word in the process label is <u>always a verb</u>. The next word or two is always the subject of the process. The subject usually includes a noun. For our example *business event* "**A Bill Arrives from a Supplier**" we have to ask ourselves, *What are we really doing here?* Since we are receiving a bill from a supplier we can name the process "Receive Bill". That gives us a strong verb and a subject.

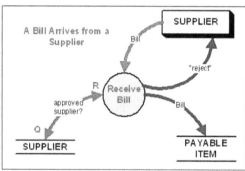

Point Form Style
1. Receive the **bill**.
2. Determine if it is from a recognized and approved **supplier**.
3. If it is, record it.
4. If the **supplier** is not recognized, reject the **bill**.

SUPPLIER
* supplier name
* supplier address
* contact name
* phone #

PAYABLE ITEM
* Due date
* Amount due

Fig. 4.41: Complete Business Process – with Object descriptions, narrative and process name

---

[10] See Chapter 3, The Business Rules Table.

Labels for processes must be strong and to the point, not abstractions. Abstractions that you want to stay away from include weak verbs such as "process" and "handle". For example, "Process Employee Pay" sounds like something we do to sausages. It's far better to say "Pay Employee". Another example of a weak label is, "Handle Payables", which sounds more like a juggling act than the more specific "Pay Supplier".

Examples of strong and pointy process labels include:

Pay Supplier
Open Account
Ship Product
Reserve Seat
Receive Loan Application
Receive Payment

Although we haven't completed the **Business Rules Table**, we have done the **Business Process Diagram**, so we can now check off this *business event* from our **Project Business Event List**.

> **Project Business Event List**
> - ~~A Bill Arrives from a Supplier~~
> - **It is Time to Pay a Supplier**

Fig. 4.42: Project Business Event List

Now that we have created a **Business Process Diagram** that describes part of the business requirement (i.e., the *essential* requirement, without defining how it will be implemented), we can proceed with the **Business Rules Table**, where we will define the remaining business requirements for this specific process.

Take the Objects that are in the "Receive Bill" **Business Process Diagram** and build up a **Business Rules Table** for those Objects, so we can ask a series of specific questions.

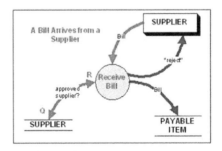

Fig. 4.43: Business Process Diagram – "Receive Bill"

Build the table by placing the Objects **SUPPLIER** and **PAYABLE ITEM** found in the diagram (Fig. 4.43) into the rows and columns indicated in Fig. 4.44. Put a '**1**' in front of each of the Objects in the anchor position to the left. This will help you focus on a single occurrence of the anchor Object when you ask the questions that arise from this table.

	BRT	Supplier	Payable Item
1	Supplier	---	
1	Payable Item		---

Fig. 4.44: Basic Structure of Business Rules Table (BRT)

For the time being, blank out the intersection of like Objects, such as **SUPPLIER+SUPPLIER** and **PAYABLE ITEM+-PAYABLE ITEM**. We'll discuss those later.

After placing each of the Objects into the **Business Rules Table** that we found in the **Business Process Diagram**, we start with the first 'anchor' Object and ask the 'BRT Questions' of it. You can usually use the verb you assigned to the process ('receive') to structure the 'BRT Questions'.

PLACEHOLDER QUESTION: **"For a single, specific SUPPLIER how many PAYABLE ITEMs might we receive?"** We don't wait for an answer to this first question. It is just a mental placeholder. We immediately go on with the three follow-on questions, soliciting a response from our subject-matter experts for each of them.

QUESTION # 1: **"Could we receive just <u>one</u> PAYABLE ITEM from the SUPPLIER?"** This question isn't intended to exclude the two following questions, but your SMEs may be tempted to respond with an expanded answer such as, *"Yes, and we might get several bills from them..."* which already answers the next question. If the answer is **NO** we enter nothing in the cell joining the two Objects that make up the question. But if the answer is **YES**, we put a '1' in the **SUPPLIER+PAYABLE ITEM** intersection cell.

BRT	Supplier	Payable Item
1 Supplier	---	1
1 Payable Item		---

Fig. 4.45: SUPPLIER + PAYABLE ITEM relationship in "Receive Bill" context

QUESTION # 2: **"Could we receive <u>many</u> PAYABLE ITEMs from the SUPPLIER?"** This kind of closed-ended question tends to draw out specific responses. Again, if the answer is **NO** we enter nothing in the cell joining the two Objects that make up the question. But if the answer is **YES**, we put an 'N' in the **SUPPLIER+PAYABLE ITEM** intersection cell (Fig. 4.46).

QUESTION # 3: **"Might we <u>never</u> receive <u>any</u> PAYABLE ITEMs from the SUPPLIER at all?"** Notice that this question does not ask, *"Could there be none..."*, which is a completely different kind of

BRT	Supplier	Payable Item
1 Supplier	---	1, N
1 Payable Item		---

Fig. 4.46: SUPPLIER + PAYABLE ITEM relationship in "Receive Bill" context

question. What we're looking for here is, firstly, an <u>exclusion</u> from the possibility of any other answers than those given to the first two 'BRT Questions'. Secondly, we're looking for the <u>inclusion</u> of a possible exception as being part of normal business policy. In other words, this question serves the dual purpose of verifying answers already given, and a search for legitimate exceptions to those answers.

When there is a **YES** to this kind of question (i.e., *"We might **never** receive a payable item from a supplier…"*) we find that SMEs often like to discuss the exceptional situation at length, as if it was a newly discovered business policy.

On the other hand, if the answer is **NO** (i.e., *"We might **not ever** receive any payable items – therefore we will always receive one or more payable items from a supplier…"*) then we enter nothing in the cell joining the two Objects that make up the question. But if the answer is **YES**, we put a '**0**' in the **SUPPLIER+PAYABLE ITEM** intersection cell.

Notice that we ask this third question from the perspective of all time; that is, the word "never" is intentionally chosen to mean just that – **never** – spanning all time. Time is an interesting element – it just keeps right on moving, no matter what we do. You certainly can substitute the words "not ever" if you wish.

BRT		Supplier	Payable Item
1	Supplier	---	1, N, 0
1	Payable Item		---

Fig. 4.47: SUPPLIER + PAYABLE ITEM relationship in "Receive Bill" context

When a client or subject matter expert answers "yes" to this third question, we must always follow up with a fourth question:

QUESTION # 4: **"Under what circumstances might that be true?"**

Let's partition this a bit more so we can understand it better.

All the suppliers that make up our **SUPPLIER** Object are "approved" suppliers. These are the only ones that are part of our list of suppliers. (It sort of makes sense that our list would not include the entire world of suppliers.)

In this example we have just asked the subject-matter expert, **"Might we never receive any PAYABLE ITEMs from the SUPPLIER at all?"** And the SME, quite reasonably replied, *"That's right, we might never receive a payable item from a supplier."*

The question, of course, is … how does someone get to become an approved supplier, and yet we don't do any business with that supplier? To find out we have to ask the follow-up question **"Under what circumstances might that be true … *that we might never get a payable item from a supplier?*"** In this example, our client's answers could be several:

"They could have gone out of business before we ordered anything from them."

"We did order from the supplier, but they were never able to ship the product to us, so eventually we just stopped doing business with them."

Both of the above, and more, are possible answers in this circumstance. It is the analyst's responsibility, and challenge, to ferret out as much information as possible from the client or subject-matter experts.

So what does it accomplish for us to uncover these "never" situations? Plain and simple, it goes directly to the issue of completeness of the business requirements. It enables us to find *business events* – situations or circumstances – that we may not have found previously. Remember that our definition of a *business event* is "… an essential business condition, a state, an external requirement, or a circumstance …" and our fourth follow-on question is **"Under what circumstances might that be true?"** In other words, with this question, we're really looking for *business events*. And a complete business requirement means finding all the *business events* the target business area must deal with.

Let's look at each of the scenarios we have painted.

1. "They could have gone out of business before we ordered anything from them."

Based on this answer we must follow up with the subject-matter experts and ask if the *business event* **"The Supplier Goes Out of Business"** is something that could be within the scope of the project. For an Accounts Payable project, it seems reasonable that we would want to know if one of our suppliers went out of business. If our subject-matter expert says, *"Yes, we would like to know"* then add this new *business event* to the **Project Business Event List (Parking Lot)**[11].

> **Project Business Event List (Parking Lot)**
> - ~~A Bill Arrives from a Supplier~~
> - **It is Time to Pay a Supplier**
> - **The Supplier Goes Out of Business**

Fig. 4.48: Business Event List 'Parking Lot' with discovered events

2. "We did order from the supplier, but they were never able to ship the product to us, so eventually we just stopped doing business with them."

From that answer we must follow up with the subject-matter expert and ask if the *business events* **"The Supplier is Unable to Fill the Product Order"** or **"Product Does Not Arrive from Supplier"** are circumstances we need to know about in our system. If so, are they within the scope of the project? If our subject-matter expert says, *"Yes, we need to know this"* then we add both new *business*

---

[11] The Project Business Event List, originally generated during the *Project Scope Blitz*, is now expanded into a Parking Lot of *business events* discovered during the detailed discovery sessions.

events to our **Project Business Event List (Parking Lot)**, in Fig. 4.49. (We'll add both *business events* because they seem to be a little different.)

Project Business Event List (Parking Lot)

- A Bill Arrives from a Supplier
- It is Time to Pay a Supplier
- The Supplier Goes Out of Business
- The Supplier is Unable to Fill the Product Order
- Product Does Not Arrive from Supplier

Fig. 4.49: Business Event List 'Parking Lot' with discovered events

There are other ways to find new *business events*, too. One of the best ways is simply by *listening* carefully to the client or SME. But listening for what? You will recall that we specified that suppliers must be "approved" before they can be on our list of suppliers. In this case we have to ask, *"How did the supplier get to be approved?"* Since it hasn't been covered yet, is there a *business event* such as "**Supplier Applies to Become an Approved Supplier**"? To find out we ask our SMEs. If their answer is, *"Yes, we receive applications from suppliers who want to become approved suppliers,"* then we add this to our list of new *business events* too, as in Fig. 4.50.

Project Business Event List (Parking Lot)

- A Bill Arrives from a Supplier
- It is Time to Pay a Supplier
- The Supplier Goes Out of Business
- The Supplier is Unable to Fill the Product Order
- Product Does Not Arrive from Supplier
- Supplier Applies to Become an Approved Supplier

Fig. 4.50: Business Event List 'Parking Lot' with discovered events

As you can see, the process of going through the 'BRT Questions' produces a lot of information that goes directly to the heart of the project. The 'BRT Questions' not only help us find business rules (we'll get to the details of that in a moment), but they help us find hidden *business events* too, like the ones above.

Let's review.

We started with two original *business events* ("**A Bill Arrives from a Supplier**" and "**It is Time to Pay a Supplier**"), supported by two Objects (**SUPPLIER** and **PAYABLE ITEM**). We also attributed some data to the two Objects; and we found several new *business events* to add to our list. We also determined the ratio of occurrences (0, 1, N) between two Objects. For the first *business event* that we worked on ("**A Bill Arrives from a Supplier**"), there now only remains the task of writing the business rules that come from the **Business Rules Table**, and to assign those rules to the right Objects.

BRT		Supplier	Payable Item
1	Supplier	---	1, N, 0
1	Payable Item		---

Fig. 4.51: SUPPLIER + PAYABLE ITEM relationship

For the first anchor Object – **SUPPLIER** – we know that we could receive one or several **PAYABLE ITEMs**, or we may never receive any at all, for which we have several examples. These rules (noted with the symbols **1,N,0**) must be documented as declarative statements in the correct context (i.e., with the proper verb) under the anchor Object **SUPPLIER**. In this example, the **PAYABLE ITEM**s rules for **SUPPLIER** might read something like you see in Fig. 4.52.

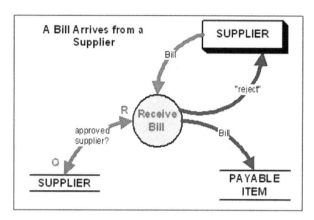

SUPPLIER

Business Rules

- We can receive one or more **PAYABLE ITEM**s from a **SUPPLIER**.

- We may never receive a **PAYABLE ITEM** from a **SUPPLIER** (e.g., may go out of business before we order a product; may not have been able to fill the only order from us).

Data Attributes

- supplier name
- supplier address
- contact name
- phone #

Fig. 4.53: Business Rules are in the context of the Process for which the BRT was built

Fig. 4.52: SUPPLIER Business Rules

The next step is to ask the 'BRT Questions' of the second anchor Object, **PAYABLE ITEM**. Let's play it out.

PLACEHOLDER QUESTION: **"For a single, specific PAYABLE ITEM that we have received, how many SUPPLIERs might it come from?"** Don't wait for an answer for this first question – it's your mental placeholder – just immediately go on with the three follow-on questions.

QUESTION # 1: **"Could the PAYABLE ITEM be from only one SUPPLIER?"** In this example the answer from our subject matter experts is, *"Yes, of course, what did you think?* So, with a **YES** answer, we put a '**1**' in the **PAYABLE ITEM+SUPPLIER** intersection cell.

BRT		Supplier	Payable Item
1	Supplier	---	1, N, 0
1	Payable Item	1	---

Fig. 4.54: PAYABLE ITEM + SUPPLIER relationship

QUESTION # 2: **"Could the PAYABLE ITEM be from several SUPPLIERs?"** Our SME tells us the answer is **NO**, so we enter nothing in the cell joining the two Objects that make up the question.

BRT	Supplier	Payable Item
1 Supplier	---	1, N, 0
1 Payable Item	1	---

Fig. 4.55: PAYABLE ITEM + SUPPLIER relationship

QUESTION # 3: **"Might the PAYABLE ITEM not be received from any SUPPLIER at all?"** Once in a while this question addresses the intuitively obvious – such as this one. Of course a payable item must come from an approved supplier, otherwise it can't be recognized as a payable item … someone else's perhaps, but not ours. Even through the answer to the question seems self-evident, we still have to confirm with our subject-matter experts. The answer, of course, is *"No"* – a payable item must come from a supplier, therefore we enter nothing new in the **PAYABLE ITEM+SUPPLIER** intersection cell.

BRT	Supplier	Payable Item
1 Supplier	---	1, N, 0
1 Payable Item	1	---

Fig. 4.56: PAYABLE ITEM + SUPPLIER relationship

Sometimes, when there is a painfully obvious answer to a question you need to ask (such as verifying that a single, specific bill can only come from one supplier), it is easier to ask the client the 'BRT Question' differently than to try to solicit a double negative to mean *"yes"*. The question **"Might the PAYABLE ITEM not be received from any SUPPLIER at all?"** can cause, at the very least, a pained quizzical look on the face of the client or subject-matter expert. As they try to process this question, they are also wondering how you could ask such a question. What is probably going through their mind is the question, *"Say what?"* A far better way of approaching this is to make a declarative statement with the answer, thus soliciting disagreement (which you probably won't get). For example, in this case, I would make the statement, **"And a PAYABLE ITEM can only come from one SUPPLIER, right?"** If they disagree, they will tell you. Otherwise, you'll get a fast nod of their collective heads and you can go on to the next questions or issues.

After you have asked the questions and got the answers, and entered them into the **Business Rules Table**, the new rules have to be written as declarative statements under the Object **PAYABLE ITEM**, which might read as in Fig. 4.57.

BRT		Supplier	Payable Item
1	Supplier	---	1, N, 0
1	Payable Item	1	---

PAYABLE ITEM
Business Rules
- A **PAYABLE ITEM** can be received from one **SUPPLIER** only.

Data Attributes
- Due date
- Amount due

Fig. 4.57: Business Rules for Payable Item

The **Business Requirements Document** – the complete set of requirements documentation – is built incrementally. We record the requirements as we go through the analysis process and discover the business requirements with our clients and subject-matter experts. This incremental approach is possible because the requirements documentation doesn't have to be written serially or like a novel. In addition to being Object-based, it is focused on the individual **Business Process Diagrams**, and each component stands on its own. Therefore, the document is not produced serially, it is created in components: *Business event*, business process, Objects, data attributes, descriptive narrative, Business Rules Table, and context-specific business rules. This, in itself, speeds up the process significantly compared to old-school approaches.

To demonstrate this progression, let's look at the second *business event* on our list, "**It is Time to Pay a Supplier**".

**Project Business Event List
(Parking Lot)**

- A Bill Arrives from a Supplier
- It is Time to Pay a Supplier
- The Supplier Goes Out of Business
- The Supplier is Unable to Fill our Product Order
- Product Does Not Arrive from Supplier
- The Product Received from the Supplier is Defective
- Supplier Applies to Become an Approved Supplier

Fig. 4.58: Business Event List 'Parking Lot' with discovered event

Once again, the first question we ask is, *"How do I know that it is time to pay a supplier?"* The answer, of course, is *"We know because we have a due date."* You will recall earlier we attributed *due date* and *amount due* to the Object **PAYABLE ITEM**. The diagram and the accompanying data would, therefore, look like this, in Fig. 4.59 and 4.60.

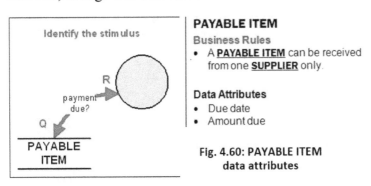

PAYABLE ITEM

Business Rules
- A **PAYABLE ITEM** can be received from one **SUPPLIER** only.

Data Attributes
- Due date
- Amount due

Fig. 4.60: PAYABLE ITEM
data attributes

Fig. 4.59: Business Process
queries 'due date' to identify if it
is time to pay supplier

This is also an example of where a stimulus that identifies a *business event* and initiates a process does not come from a Terminator, but instead comes from data that's part of an Object. This is the most common way of identifying if "**It is Time …**" for something.

The second question is, *"What are we going to do about it?"* In this example our client told us that we pay the balance of the account after calculating any previous payments that were made to the supplier. Therefore, we must first determine if any previous payments to the supplier have been made.

To know if there were any previous payments we must have an Object called **PAYMENT**. Its data attributes would include *amount paid* (which includes previous payments), *date paid* and *method of payment*. There could be several previous payments.

PAYMENT

Data Attributes
- Amount paid
- Date paid
- Method of payment

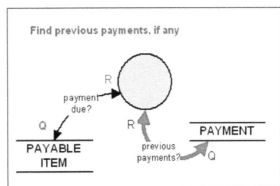

Fig. 4.61: Business Process Diagram and Object
data – finding previous payments

After we determined if there were any previous payments, we can calculate the remaining balance that's due.

We also need to identify the **SUPPLIER** we're going to send the payment to; and we can find that supplier by locating which one is linked[12] to the **PAYABLE ITEM**.

Fig. 4.62: Business Process identifies Supplier

And then we can send the payment to the supplier.

Fig. 4.63: Business Process issues payment to supplier

---

[12] Using the **PAYABLE ITEM**'s *foreign key* to find it.

The last question to our subject matter expert is, *"What do we need to record or remember about this process?"* In this example we want to remember the payment sent to the supplier, including the method of payment and when it was made. We can draw this as illustrated in our diagram below (Fig. 4.64). The data attributes for the **PAYMENT** Object are also listed below.

PAYMENT

Data Attributes
- Amount paid
- Date paid
- Method of payment

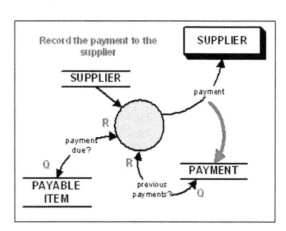

Fig. 4.64: Business Process remembers payment issued

This now leaves us with a complete **Business Process Diagram** for the *business event* "**It is Time to Pay a Supplier**" (as shown in Fig. 4.65). But, once again, lots of things haven't been done yet: We still haven't named the process; nor have we written a descriptive narrative. We have only done a little bit of data attribution; and we haven't completed the **Business Rules Table** to define our business rules for the new Object, **PAYMENT**.

The very first question about this *business event* to our subject-matter experts was, *"How do I*

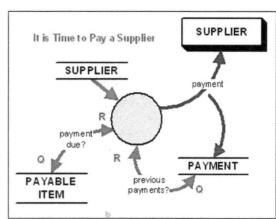

Fig. 4.65: Business Process almost done

know that it is time to pay a supplier?" This resulted in finding the stimulus (there was a *due date* for the **PAYABLE ITEM**), which eventually led to the full diagram.

As you draw the diagram for the process, your discussions with the subject-matter experts tend to bring out the remaining Objects and the data that make up the Objects. In this particular example, there are no more Objects or data needed to support the *business event* "**It is Time to Pay a Supplier**".

The next step is to write a descriptive narrative of the **Business Process Diagram**. The narrative has to be clear, concise, unambiguous, in plain business language – and brief.

So far, we have left the bubble that represents the process unlabeled. The process name is only assigned after we have written the narrative necessary to support the diagram.

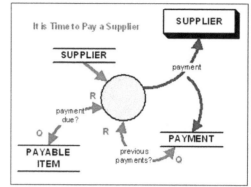

Our objective is to write a narrative that explains the **Business Process Diagram** in as much detail as necessary, but no more. Our narrative must be in plain language, without any technobabble. The end result must be a

Fig. 4.66: Business Process needs a descriptive narrative

narrative that's easily understood by the client, subject-matter experts, and a technical team.

We determine the narrative needed by identifying the tasks associated with each data flow that comes into or goes out of the process. For our "**It is Time to Pay a Supplier**" *business event* example, it looks like the illustration in Fig. 4.67;

although we don't draw those little nodes on our real documentation, we just write the narratives.

Each of these nodes must be referenced in some way in the narrative that you write. You can use at least two different styles when producing your narrative, the Structured Narrative Style, or the Point Form Style. You can also develop your own style, as long as your narrative text

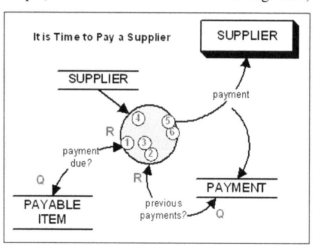

Fig. 4.67: Nodes identify tasks to be part of descriptive narrative

refers to each of the data flows entering or leaving the process. You may have to add additional text to describe the transformation of data, such as calculations or other formulas.

To write a narrative in this way is relatively easy and without pain. It enables you to quickly determine the tasks that make up a process without getting writer's block. Both types of narratives have been done for this example.

Point Form Style

1. Find bills (**PAYABLE ITEM**s) that are due to be paid.
2. Find previous **PAYMENT**s that have been made against individual bills (**PAYABLE ITEM**s), if any.
3. Determine the amount to be paid to a **SUPPLIER** (*amount due* minus previous *amount paid*).
4. Locate the **SUPPLIER** for the **PAYABLE ITEM**.
5. Pay the **SUPPLIER**.
6. Record the **PAYMENT**.

Structured Narrative Style

For each bill (**PAYABLE ITEM**) that is due for payment, determine the balance to be paid based on previous partial **PAYMENT**s against the bill. Pay the **SUPPLIER** and remember the **PAYMENT**.

Fig. 4.67(a): Two styles of process narratives

We now have a complete diagram and narrative for the *business event* "**It is Time to Pay a Supplier**". We have also identified the Objects and data attributes we need to support the process.

But we haven't named the process yet, which is the last thing we do before we build out the **Business Rules Table** for this process.

You will recall that a *business event* name (such as "**It is Time to Pay a Supplier**") never starts with a verb. The name of the process that supports a *business event*, however, always starts with a verb.

So what are we really doing in this process? We're sending a payment to a supplier; therefore, we can name the process "Pay Supplier". That gives us a strong verb and a subject.

Although we haven't completed the **Business Rules Table** for the new **PAYMENT** Object yet, we can now check off this *business event* from our **Project Business Event List (Parking Lot)**,

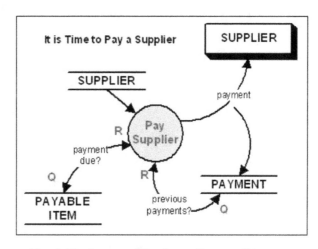

Fig. 4.68: A named Business Process Diagram

Project Business Event List (Parking Lot)

- A Bill Arrives from a Supplier
- It is Time to Pay a Supplier
- **The Supplier Goes Out of Business**
- **The Supplier is Unable to Fill our Product Order**
- **Product Does Not Arrive from Supplier**
- **Supplier Applies to Become an Approved Supplier**

Fig. 4.69: Making progress against the Business Event List 'Parking Lot'

The **Business Rules Table** has to include all Objects that support a process. Although we did work through a BRT for the earlier process "Receive Bill" the context has now changed, so there will be different rules produced from the table. Therefore, all Objects that support the process "Pay Supplier" must be queried.

Take the Objects that are in the diagram for the "Pay Supplier" process and build up a **Business Rules Table** for those Objects.

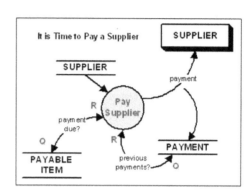

Fig. 4.70: Business Process Diagram – "Pay Supplier"

Build a table, just like the previous example, by placing the Objects (**SUPPLIER**, **PAYABLE ITEM** and **PAYMENT**) in the rows and columns indicated. Put a '**1**' in front of each of the Objects in the anchor position to the left. This will help you focus on a single occurrence of the anchor Object when you ask the questions that arise from this table.

For the time being, blank out the intersection of like Objects.

	BRT	Supplier	Payable Item	Payment
1	Supplier	---		
1	Payable Item		---	
1	Payment			---

Fig. 4.71: Business Rules Table for process "Pay Supplier"

We can now start with the first 'anchor' Object and ask the 'BRT Questions'. You can usually use the verb you assigned to the business process (Fig. 4.70) to structure your 'BRT Questions'. If that verb doesn't work, then select another verb construct based on the concept behind the process. The idea is to ask the 'BRT Questions' based on the context of the process.

PLACEHOLDER QUESTION: **"For a single, specific SUPPLIER how many PAYABLE ITEMs might be due to be paid to them?"** We don't wait for an answer to this first question. It is just a mental placeholder. We immediately go on with the three follow-on questions, soliciting a response from our subject-matter experts for each of them.

QUESTION # 1: **"Could there be just <u>one</u> <u>PAYABLE ITEM</u> due to be paid to a <u>SUPPLIER</u>?"** Our SME answers, *"Yes, and there might be several bills to be paid to a supplier too…"* which already answers the next question. Since the answer is **YES**, we put a **'1'** in the <u>SUPPLIER+PAYABLE ITEM</u> intersection cell.

	BRT	Supplier	Payable Item	Payment
1	Supplier	---	1	
1	Payable Item		---	
1	Payment			---

Fig. 4.72: SUPPLIER + PAYABLE ITEM relationship in "Pay Supplier" context

QUESTION # 2: **"Could there be <u>many</u> <u>PAYABLE ITEM</u>s due to be paid to a <u>SUPPLIER</u>?"** The answer is **YES**, so we put an **'N'** in the <u>SUPPLIER-PAYABLE ITEM</u> intersection cell.

	BRT	Supplier	Payable Item	Payment
1	Supplier	---	1, N	
1	Payable Item		---	
1	Payment			---

Fig. 4.73: SUPPLIER + PAYABLE ITEM relationship in "Pay Supplier" context

QUESTION # 3: **"Might we <u>never</u> have <u>any</u> <u>PAYABLE ITEM</u>s that are due to be paid to a <u>SUPPLIER</u> at all?"** The answer is **YES**, so we put a **'0'** in the <u>SUPPLIER-PAYABLE ITEM</u> intersection cell.

	BRT	Supplier	Payable Item	Payment
1	Supplier	---	1, N, 0	
1	Payable Item		---	
1	Payment			---

Fig. 4.74: SUPPLIER + PAYABLE ITEM relationship in "Pay Supplier" context

When the answer is "yes" to this third question, we must always follow up with a fourth question:

QUESTION # 4: **"Under what circumstances might that be true?"**

"They could have gone out of business before we ordered anything from them."

"We did order from the supplier, but they were never able to ship the product to us, so eventually we just stopped doing business with them."

These are the same responses we got when we asked the SMEs about the **SUPPLIER+PAYABLE ITEM** relationship in the context of the **"Receive Bill"** process earlier. That being the case, we don't have to add any new *business events* to our list since they have all been added before.

BRT	Supplier	Payable Item	Payment
1 Supplier	---	1, N, 0	
1 Payable Item		---	
1 Payment			---

Fig. 4.75: SUPPLIER + PAYABLE ITEM relationship in "Pay Supplier" context

Now we need to write the business rules for the new relationship (based on context of the "Pay Supplier" process, Fig. 4.76) between **SUPPLIER** and **PAYABLE ITEM**.

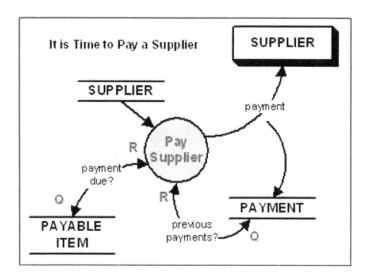

Fig. 4.76: Business Process Diagram – "Pay Supplier"

For the first anchor Object – **SUPPLIER** – we now know that we could issue a payment for one or several **PAYABLE ITEM**s, or we may never pay any at all. These rules are documented as declarative statements under the anchor Object **SUPPLIER** (in the context of the "Pay Supplier" business process it supports). In this example, the **PAYABLE ITEM**s rules attributed to **SUPPLIER** might read something like those in Fig. 4.77.

SUPPLIER

Business Rules
- We can receive one or more **PAYABLE ITEM**s from a **SUPPLIER**.

- We may never receive a **PAYABLE ITEM** from a **SUPPLIER** (e.g., may go out of business before we order a product; may have sent us a defective product on their only order from us; may not have been able to fill the only order from us).

- ★ We can pay one or more **PAYABLE ITEM**s for a **SUPPLIER**.

- ★ We may never have a **PAYABLE ITEM** to pay for a **SUPPLIER** (e.g., may go out of business before we order a product; may not have been able to fill the only order from us).

Data Attributes
- supplier name
- supplier address
- contact name
- phone #

Fig. 4.77: SUPPLIER Business Rules

The next step is to ask the 'BRT Questions' of the next Object (**PAYMENT**) that intersect with the anchor Object **SUPPLIER**. Let's play this one out.

PLACEHOLDER QUESTION: **"For a single, specific SUPPLIER how many PAYMENTs might we issue (pay) to them?"** We don't wait for an answer to this first question.

QUESTION # 1: **"Could we issue just one PAYMENT to a SUPPLIER?"** Our SME answers, *"Yes, we might only ever make one payment to a supplier…"*. Put a **'1'** in the **SUPPLIER+PAYMENT** intersection cell.

	BRT	Supplier	Payable Item	Payment
1	Supplier	---	1, N, 0	1
1	Payable Item		---	
1	Payment			---

Fig. 4.78: SUPPLIER + PAYMENT relationship in "Pay Supplier" context

QUESTION # 2: **"Could we issue <u>many</u> <u>PAYMENT</u>s to a <u>SUPPLIER</u>?"** The answer is **YES**, so we put an **'N'** in the <u>**SUPPLIER+PAYMENT**</u> intersection cell.

BRT		Supplier	Payable Item	Payment
1	Supplier	---	1, N, 0	1, N
1	Payable Item		---	
1	Payment			---

Fig. 4.79: SUPPLIER + PAYMENT relationship in "Pay Supplier" context

QUESTION # 3: **"Might we never issue <u>any</u> <u>PAYMENT</u>s to a <u>SUPPLIER</u> at all?"** The answer is **YES**, so we put a **'0'** in the <u>**SUPPLIER+PAYMENT**</u> intersection cell.

BRT		Supplier	Payable Item	Payment
1	Supplier	---	1, N, 0	1, N, 0
1	Payable Item		---	
1	Payment			---

Fig. 4.80: SUPPLIER + PAYMENT relationship in "Pay Supplier" context

When the answer is "yes"
to this question, we always follow up with a fourth question:

QUESTION # 4: **"Under what circumstances might that be true?"**

"While they were on our list of approved suppliers, we just never ordered anything from them."

There may be other reason, too, but we won't list them here.

This circumstance begs the question, *"Do we need to know about those suppliers who don't do business with us after a certain period of time?"* The answer from our subject-matter expert was *"No, we don't care,"* so we don't have to add any new *business events* to our list on the right.

Project Business Event List (Parking Lot)
- ~~A Bill Arrives from a Supplier~~
- ~~It is Time to Pay a Supplier~~
- The Supplier Goes Out of Business
- The Supplier is Unable to Fill our Product Order
- Product Does Not Arrive from Supplier
- Supplier Applies to Become an Approved Supplier

Fig. 4.81: The Project Business Event List 'Parking Lot'

Now we need to write the business rules for the new relationship between **SUPPLIER** and **PAYMENT**. The **PAYMENT** rules attributed to **SUPPLIER** might read something like what you see in Fig. 4.82.

SUPPLIER

Business Rules

★ We can issue one or more **PAYMENT**s to a **SUPPLIER**.

★ We may never issue a **PAYMENT** to a **SUPPLIER** (e.g., we just didn't order anything from them).

Fig. 4.82: More SUPPLIER Business Rules

You go through exactly the same process for the other Objects that support the process "Pay Supplier", those Objects being **PAYABLE ITEM** and **PAYMENT**. When you're done, and you have all the answers to the questions, you will end up with the following entries in the **Business Rules Table**.

	BRT	Supplier	Payable Item	Payment
1	Supplier	---	1, N, 0	1, N, 0
1	Payable Item	1	---	1, N
1	Payment	1	1	---

Fig. 4.83: Business Rules Table (BRT) for "Pay Supplier" process

The answers in the BRT spell out policy quite nicely:

★ A specific **PAYABLE ITEM** can be from one **SUPPLIER** only. (Makes sense.)
★ A specific **PAYABLE ITEM** can have one or several **PAYMENT**s made against it. (In effect, this says there can be partial payments.)
★ A specific **PAYMENT** can only be issued to one **SUPPLIER**. (This, too, makes sense.)
★ A specific **PAYMENT** can only be for one **PAYABLE ITEM**. (This is because, in our example, accounting is done on an open item basis rather than balance forward.)

All of these rules are attributed to their respective anchor Objects.

Earlier I asked you to blank out the intersection of like objects, such as the cells for **SUPPLIER+SUPPLIER**, **PAYABLE ITEM+PAYABLE ITEM** and **PAYMENT+PAYMENT**. That's because if we ask the same questions of these recursive relationships[13] as we would of all the other Objects, we would find it very challenging. For example, for the "Pay Supplier" process, the series of 'BRT Questions' for **PAYABLE ITEM** would read as follows:

PLACEHOLDER QUESTION: **"For a single, specific PAYABLE ITEM how many other PAYABLE ITEMs might we pay for?"** Say what? This doesn't seem to make a lot of sense.

QUESTION # 1: **"Could we pay for just one PAYABLE ITEM ... PAYABLE ITEM?"** How do we even structure this question? There's clearly a problem here.

QUESTION # 2: **"Could we pay for many PAYABLE ITEMs .... PAYABLE ITEM?"** Again, how do we even structure this question? This isn't working.

QUESTION # 3: **"Might we never pay any PAYABLE ITEMs ... PAYABLE ITEM at all?"** What kind of sentence structure could we use to make this into a sensible question?

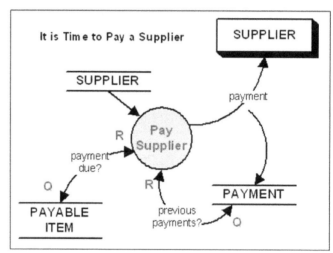

Fig. 4.84: Business Process Diagram "Pay Supplier"

Of course, none of those questions work in this context – and they usually don't work when trying to ask questions about the relationship between like Objects. So how do we ask these important questions?

---

[13] A recursive relationship occurs when there is a relationship between an Object and itself. For example, a one-to-many recursive relationship occurs when an **EMPLOYEE** is the manager of other **EMPLOYEE**s. In that scenario, the **EMPLOYEE** Object is related to itself, and there is a one-to-many relationship between one **EMPLOYEE** (the manager) and many other **EMPLOYEE**s (the people who report to the manager).

By changing how we ask.

BRT		Supplier	Payable Item	Payment
1	Supplier	---	1, N, 0	1, N, 0
1	Payable Item	1	---	1, N
1	Payment	1	1	---

Fig. 4.85: The remaining questions to ask in a Business Rules Table (BRT) for the "Pay Supplier" process

If you are querying the intersection of like Objects – or even if the standard 'BRT Questions' just don't seem to work or don't make too much sense – then change how you ask the placeholder question to the following (in a "Pay Supplier" context):

SUPPLIER Substitute Placeholder Question: **"If I know about one SUPPLIER that we pay, under what circumstances would I ever want to find another, related SUPPLIER that we pay?**

PAYABLE ITEM Substitute Placeholder Question: **"If I know about one PAYABLE ITEM that we pay for, under what circumstances would I ever want to find another, related PAYABLE ITEM that we pay for?**

Fig. 4.86: Business Process Diagram – "Pay Supplier"

PAYMENT Substitute Placeholder Question: **"If I know about one PAYMENT that is issued to a supplier, under what circumstances would I ever want to find another, related PAYMENT to that supplier?**

The difference between this substitute placeholder Question and the regular one is that we <u>do</u> expect an answer from our subject-matter experts.

With this question, we are looking for a *circumstance* – which, as we know, is really a *business event*. The answers that our SMEs give us identify *business events* (circumstances) that may or may not already be on our **Project Business Event List (Parking Lot)**. Answers such as, *"We want to know about multiple payments to a supplier so we can determine how much business we're giving them"* will lead to a new *business event*, **"Company Wants to Know Historical Payments to a Supplier (for a Period)"**. If this *business event* – regardless of how it is stated – is already on the **Project Business Event List (Parking Lot)**, there's nothing to add to the list. If it's not, however, a new *business event* has been discovered and it has to be added to the list if it is determined to be in scope.

Once you have the answer to the <u>substitute placeholder question</u>, the regular three (or four) '<u>BRT Questions</u>' still have to be asked of the subject Object.

Can the discovery of a *business event* lead to additional questions that, in turn, can find other *business events*? You bet. A good example is the answer we just looked at.

The new *business event*, "**Company Wants to Know Historical Payments to a Supplier (for a Period)**" is essentially a report, regardless of the form it will finally take. Any time a report or a list is required, the question an analyst must ask is, *"If I know about the historical payments we made to a supplier, what does that tell us?"*

Earlier we looked at <u>Inclusion Questions</u> for Objects and data items. This same kind of question can be applied to potentially discover new *business events* from already identified *business events*.

Project Business Event List (Parking Lot)
• A Bill Arrives from a Supplier
• It is Time to Pay a Supplier
• The Supplier Goes Out of Business
• The Supplier is Unable to Fill our Product Order
• Product Does Not Arrive from Supplier
• Supplier Applies to Become an Approved Supplier
• Company Wants to Know Historical Payments to a Supplier (for a Period)

Fig. 4.87: The Project Event List 'Parking Lot' with another event added

The Inclusion Question (for Events)
"**If we know about {**<u>the EVENT</u>**} what will it <u>enable</u> us to do that we could not do if we didn't know about it?**"

The Exclusion Question (for Events)
"**If we <u>do not know</u> about {**<u>the EVENT</u>**} what will it *prevent* us from doing that we must be able to do?**"

What kind of answers might you get?

INCLUSION: "**If we know about {**<u>the historical payments to a supplier (for a period)</u>**} what will it <u>enable</u> us to do that we could not do if we didn't know about it?**" Answer: *"It enables us to do comparative research of how much business we're doing with certain suppliers so we can negotiate better financial terms with some of them."*

EXCLUSION: "**If we do not know about {**<u>the historical payments to a supplier (for a period)</u>**} what will it <u>prevent</u> us from doing that we must be able to**

do?" Same answer, different perspective: *"It would prevent us from knowing how much business we're doing with certain suppliers, which would in turn prevent us from negotiating better financial terms with some of them."*

Both answers suggest another *business event* not previously discovered, "**It is Time to Negotiate Better Financial Terms with a Supplier**", which must be added to our list.

When an identified *business event* is essentially a report or a list of some kind – regardless of how it will actually be designed and implemented – you must take it one more step and ask *"What does that tell us?"* or *"What does it prevent us from doing if we don't have it?"*

Project Business Event List (Parking Lot)
• ~~A Bill Arrives from a Supplier~~
• ~~It is Time to Pay a Supplier~~
• The Supplier Goes Out of Business
• The Supplier is Unable to Fill our Product Order
• Product Does Not Arrive from Supplier
• Supplier Applies to Become an Approved Supplier
• Company Wants to Know Historical Payments to a Supplier (for a Period)
• It is Time to Negotiate Better Financial Terms with a Supplier

Fig. 4.88: The Project Event List 'Parking Lot' with another event added

Finding reports or lists to be produced is one of the easier things to do. Clients and SMEs will always have a long list of lists and reports they want. For a consultant to simply accept a requirement for a list or report is not analysis, it's just regurgitation of what the subject matter-expert thinks should be done. But please note that the SME is not a 'business systems analyst' nor a consultant. You are. And you are the one that has to do the analysis to find out what the real requirements are, rather than the surface requirements. And a report or list is a surface requirement because people *do something* with reports, usually to uncover other information that's not directly on the report. While this isn't always the case, it often is.

Finally, from our two starting *business events* ("**A Bill Arrives from a Supplier**" and "**It is Time to Pay a Supplier**") we managed to get all of this:

1. Two **Business Process Diagrams** (Receive Bill and Pay Supplier).
2. A descriptive narrative for each of the two business processes.
3. Discovery of three Objects (**PAYABLE ITEM**, **SUPPLIER** and **PAYMENT**).
4. The necessary data attributes for each of the three Objects.
5. Business rules for each of the three Objects.
6. A list of six (6) additional *business events* that had not been found originally.

As an added benefit, we also got a prescription for database design (the required data accesses) based on the business requirements[14].

---

[14] The notation (0,1,N) in the **Business Rules Table** translates easily into the accesses required in a Conceptual Data Model, while the Objects with data attributes provides the composition of the data model.

Object-Relationship Diagrams

The examples we worked through were all **Business Process Diagrams**. Could we have developed **Object-Relationship Diagrams**[15] instead? Yes, we could have. However, it's more difficult to determine the process required for an object model than for a process model, mostly because we don't see the flow of data, we only see the relationship of Objects. It's also more difficult to get SMEs on board, since they are accustomed to working with the process activity, not a simplified static view of data. In the end, however, everything would be the same except the diagrams.

A Bill Arrives from a Supplier

Fig. 4.89: Object-Relationship Diagram for Business Event "Bill Arrives from Supplier"

It is Time to Pay a Supplier

Fig. 4.90: Object-Relationship Diagram for the Business Event "It is Time to Pay a Supplier"

4.4 The Non-Serial Incremental Approach

Business requirements for any project are developed incrementally, but it certainly should not be done serially. Using the approach in this book, you can uncover the processes, data and business rules for any *business event* at any time, in any sequence. Each can stand on its own during discovery sessions. Although many Objects are shared by different business processes, there isn't any dependency by one process on another; therefore, the sequence with which you analyze the different *business events* is unimportant. The only thing that matters is your comfort level with the sequence in which you work.

Most organizations with business systems are mature, integrated and complex; therefore, there isn't just one 'beginning' for the consultant on a project. There could be many 'beginnings', depending on the number of business areas involved and on their perspectives. Most projects in mature organizations involve several business areas; therefore, there are often as many perspectives on where things begin and end, as there are business areas represented.

This non-serial approach to analysis is also possible because the **Business Requirements Document** doesn't have to be written sequentially either. The document that's produced to define the business requirements, just like the business, should not be a serial description of business processes, like the old

---

[15] See section 1.3: The Different Diagramming Conventions.

manufacturing or paper flow systems from the past. In today's world, that would be difficult to produce, although I see that many people still try. The document you produce will be organized by *business event* (business condition), which is then a whole lot easier to read and understand.

Below is a diagram to illustrate what needs to be done to develop a business process and identify required Objects.

Develop a Business Process <u>and</u> Identify Business Objects

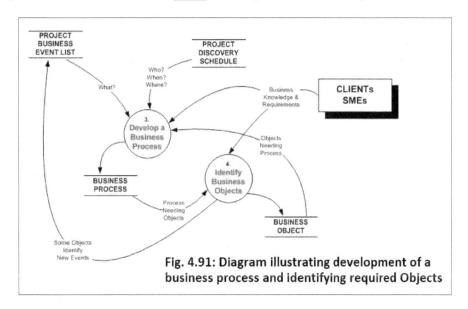

Fig. 4.91: Diagram illustrating development of a business process and identifying required Objects

After a **Business Process Diagram** has been developed to represent requirements, including the Objects that are needed, the **Business Rules Table** must be queried in the context of the business process.

Query a Business Rules Table

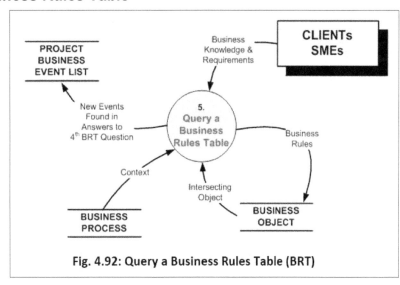

Fig. 4.92: Query a Business Rules Table (BRT)

4.5 The Object-Task Table

The **Object-Task Table** helps you find *business events* that may have been missed.

This table lists all the Objects used in a project, and indicates whether the Objects have been created, viewed, modified (sometimes) and/or removed (deleted or archived). These four tasks represent the full life-cycle of an Object. Since an Object must appear more than once in any business scenario, this table helps to determine if we have identified all the scenarios in which each Object participates. An Object such as **CUSTOMER**, for example, that is viewed only (e.g., by looking up a *customer name* and *email address*) and not referenced in any other way, clearly begs at least three questions: (1) *Under what circumstances was it created?* (2) *Is it ever modified (updated)?* (3) *Under what circumstances is it removed?*

The **Object-Task Table** is a working tool only. It does not make up part of the business requirements documentation. In other words, this table does not become part of the **Business Requirements Document**.

The **Object-Task Table** is only used after all discovery sessions with clients and SMEs have been done for your project, including diagrams, narratives and all the **Business Rules Tables**. Its purpose is only to find *business events* that were missed.

The **Object-Task Table** looks like the one below (Fig. 4.93). The Objects that populate the table are found in the **Business Process Diagrams** that were worked up for the project.

	OBJECT-TASK TABLE			
primary functions →	Create	View	Change	Retire
Product	✓	✓	✓	✓
Supplier		✓		
Payable item	✓			
Payment	✓	✓		

Fig. 4.93: An Object-Task Table

By listing all the Objects that are part of your project and then reviewing each process diagram that supports the individual *business events*, you can then determine if the Objects have been created, viewed, changed (sometimes) and/or retired (deleted or archived)[16].

---

[16] The data that make up some Objects, such as long-term statistical or research data, may never be removed if the data is part of a metric database. However, this is the exception to the rule. Most Objects are eventually archived, such as expired **CONTRACT**s or removed **SUPPLIER**s.

If an Object has not had a full life-cycle in your project, then it must be 'completed' in another. An example of this is an Object such as **SUPPLIER**. To be part of your project, **SUPPLIER** must be created somewhere, viewed (so we can see what it contains, such as a *supplier address*), perhaps changed or

updated, and finally retired or archived. If all of this has not been done with a specific Object, such as **SUPPLIER**, then we have missed a *business event*. The only question is whether the missed *business event* is inside the scope of your project, or if it belongs to another project or system. In either case, it must be documented accordingly, so project people will know that it has been addressed.

Fig. 4.94: A Business Process Diagram for the event "A Bill Arrives from a Supplier"

In the context of *your* project, the **Object-Task Table** shows clearly what is missing for any Object. If one of your project's Objects has not been created, then how can you possibly view or update it?[17]

---

[17] This is very similar to the poorly named 'CRUD matrix' (create, retrieve, update, delete), which results in the *Business Transaction Model*. This was developed by Haim Kilov, and presented at the First International Conference on Systems Integration, 1990, in a paper entitled *"From semantic to object-oriented data modeling"*. Just like the Object-Task Table, the Business Transaction Model correlates the major business processes with the general entities (Objects) defined in what they call the Enterprise Data Model. So, we're not so far apart here. The term CRUD, however, is unacceptable to me since it incorrectly implies the analysis is of little value.

Chapter 5. The Business Requirements Document – How to Package the Requirements

Contents

Up to this point we have focused on the information required to create a business requirements specification at the *business event* level. We have approached the target business areas and partitioned the analysis effort into small and manageable pieces. Now that we know what processes and data are needed to support the *business events* within the project's scope, we can package this information for distribution and future use.

5.1 The Business Interfaces Diagram

The <u>Business Interfaces Diagram</u> (also sometimes known as the "Context Diagram") identifies the interface communications needed between the target project and its outside world, without dictating the specifics of the technology to be employed.

The <u>Business Interfaces Diagram</u> is a powerful tool to graphically illustrate communication needs between the business areas in your project and its outside world. The whole diagram fits nicely on a single page, although a diagram for a project in real life can sometimes get quite busy. But, because it fits on a page, you can present and describe the whole business system in just a few minutes. Senior management generally really likes presentations you can make against this diagram.

To build this diagram, first just draw a big circle representing the target system. Put the project's name inside the circle.

Then go back and look at the individual **Business Process Diagrams** for the project. On each diagram, find the Terminator (if there is one)[18] and the data

Fig. 5.1: TORDIS Project Context bubble – The starting point

---

[18] Not all Business Process Diagrams will have a Terminator.

flow that either comes from or goes to that Terminator. Add the data flows to the Business Interfaces Diagram.

For example, the diagram on the right (Fig. 5.2) has only one Terminator (**Hospital**) and two data flows connected to it: one coming from the **Hospital** as a source of information (the *organ request*); and the other providing information to the **Hospital** (*"non-member reject"*). Add these two data flows to the Business Interfaces Diagram (Fig. 5.3, below).

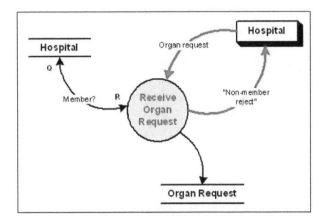

Fig. 5.2: A Business Process with data flows to & from Terminator identified

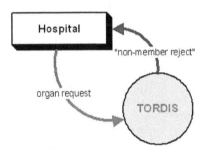

Fig. 5.3: Building up the Business Interfaces Diagram

After adding the data flows coming from and going to the **Hospital** Terminator, the TORDIS Business Interfaces Diagram will look like the picture on the immediate left (Fig. 5.3).

Using another process diagram – *Receive Organ* – Fig. 5.4, we have one new data flow to add to the Business Interfaces Diagram, which now would look like the diagram on the next page (Fig. 5.5).

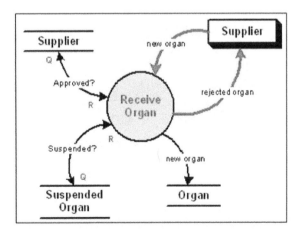

Fig. 5.4: Business Process with data flows to & from a Terminator

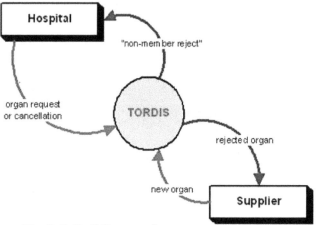

**Fig. 5.5: Building up the
Business Interfaces Diagram**

By going through each of the **Business Process Diagrams** for a project, and identifying each data flow from or to a Terminator, we end up with a <u>Business Interfaces Diagram</u> that could look like this example for the TORDIS project below (Fig. 5.6).

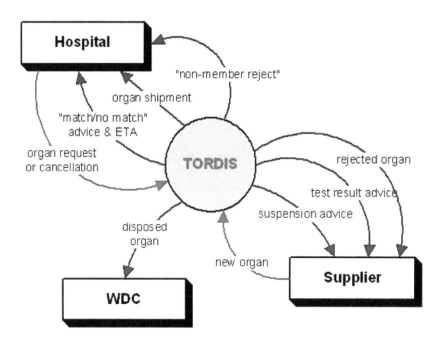

Fig. 5.6: TORDIS Project Business Interfaces Diagram

This diagram is now easily explained and presented to your clients or senior management. You can "talk through" each of the data flows that come into and leave TORDIS; and you can explain what happens inside it. The diagram clearly shows the interfaces with the outside world that need technology applied, and who is involved.

5.2 How to Package the Business Requirements

The finished **Business Requirements Document** will include the following:

* ★ **Business Interfaces Diagram** – a single picture to identity outside interfaces.
* ★ **Business Process Diagrams** – the individual business processes, with accompanying documentation.

You may be surprised at how little documentation this seems to be. First, that's because it's a business requirements specification, not a software engineering specification. Business requirements can be lean, brief and succinct without missing a thing. Second, when you take a close look at the components of the business requirements, you find it is very dense with all kinds of information: The process model has clear narratives, participating Objects, data items, and business rules that succinctly specify system behavior. The absence of technology and an implementation bias enable the document to be quite small, and to be completed very quickly.

Being the highest-level view, the Business Interfaces Diagram illustrates the communications interfaces needed between the outside world[19] and the project's business area(s). It can be used as the foundation for a communication and/or transportation network with suppliers, vendors, partners, banks, and even customers.

The individual **Business Process Diagrams** and their accompanying documentation describe the required processes and the data that supports those processes, without referring to any specific technology architecture or solution design.

The **Business Requirements Document** can be produced as a complete document or as a partial document – specific to a business area – and issued to those who should have it.

---

[19] The project's "outside world" can be internal or external to the organization.

How to Bring an Agile Approach to the Development and Distribution of Project Documentation

Traditionally, software acquisition or system design doesn't start until all the business requirements analysis has been completed. And that's a bit of a problem. In most cases, that's a very long time and is very frustrating for management who really want to get on with "the real work": Implementing the software.

To create an even bigger challenge, once all the business requirements analysis has been completed, there's the approval process. In some organizations, this can be a painful process, fraught with the politics of budgets and turf. In other organizations, the people signing off on business requirements simply look at the (conventional) size of the document (*War and Peace* comes to mind) before grumbling their consent without actually reading the document. I can't blame them.

To send out a document that details all the business requirements to everyone who was involved in the project – to all the stakeholders – and to do this after all the work has been done does not seem to be in keeping with the principles of a modern business nor that of a lean, agile organization.

This is, quite frankly, exactly how it was done in 1970. It's difficult to get better results with methods that are from a previous century. I would suggest it's time to change.

Let's face it – this old-school approach is contrary to quality management principles, too. The approval process is, after all, a way of managing the quality of the product; and, as such, should be an integral part of the business requirements process itself. To go through a major "approval" at the end of the process, for the first time, seems like a recipe for failure to me.

In a mature organization, it's quite common that stakeholders for a project could number 30 or more – perhaps many more – people.

Imagine for a moment a project that has 30 stakeholders and subject-matter experts involved in a project. Imagine also that the Financial Management group on the project is directly involved with only 12 *business events*. The Reservation area team is involved in only 7 of the project's *business events*. Product Testing is involved with 3 *events* … and a few other groups are involved in various other *events*. No one, not one business unit, is involved in or concerned with all the *business events*.

That kind of distribution of stakeholders is pretty well normal for any project.

That being the case, why should we distribute the entire document to everyone? The Financial Management area has nothing to do with a *business event* like "**It is Time to Test an Organ for Disease**"; nor is it their responsibility to review and approve the business processes required by another business area.

A **Business Requirements Document** can potentially consist of scores of pages.[20] But, if a business area is involved in only a part of the project (which is almost always the case), their willingness to wade through all the pages of a document could be very low. On the other hand, there are those who want to see everything that's documented for the project, but they really have little to do with it all. These folks sometimes get in the way and delay progress.

On scores of projects, we have found that it can be very productive to issue a subset of the **Business Requirements Document** to the different stakeholders and subject-matter experts involved, rather than the whole thing to everyone. For example, for the Product Testing area of the TORDIS project, we could create a **Business Requirements Document** that consists of the following components.

A **Business Interfaces Diagram** ('Context Diagram') showing the required interfaces with the system's outside world.

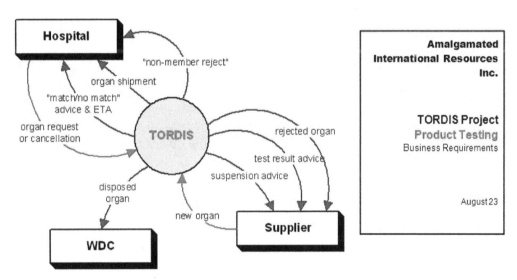

Fig. 5.6: TORDIS Project Business Interfaces Diagram

---

[20] Traditionally, the size of the finished document is a function of the complexity of the project and the number of people involved. This is not the case for event-based projects, as described in this book. The size of the finished **Business Requirements Document** is entirely a function of the number of *business events* and the number of Objects that support the business processes. This makes event-based project documentation much smaller than conventional documentation; thus much more "agile" in context.

Individual Business Process Diagrams showing the processes that belong to the business area for which the document has been prepared. (In this example, there are only three Product Testing processes.) Business process documentation must include – as well as the diagrams – descriptive narratives, Object definitions, data attributes and business rules for the Objects that support the business area the document is focused on.

Fig. 5.8: The 3 Product Testing business processes

By partitioning the **Business Requirements Document** in this manner we not only increase the focus, but we significantly reduce the volume of reading required by the clients and subject-matter experts in any business area. This can lead to faster and better turnaround. It certainly minimizes any potential distractions.

There's another important factor: The **Business Requirements Document** could only be produced with the knowledge contributed by the subject-matter experts. They participate in and contributed actively in detailed discovery sessions, and they are probably very aware of what they contributed. Their contribution is reflected in the pages of this document; and the document – when it issued by separate business areas – is clearly focused on the knowledge about that business area, without the distractions of all the other contributions by other SMEs from other areas. And since the document is theirs – and most people don't disagree with themselves – they will probably pay far better attention to the document than if it is a variety show of all the different business areas.

However, to take this idea to an even higher level of responsiveness and "agile", I suggest the following strategy.

Discovery sessions with subject-matter experts are conducted on the basis of one or more specific *business events*.[21] For each *business event*, you will create a **Business Process Diagram**. You'll do the process diagram, identify supporting Objects, attribute data items to the Objects, and determine business rules specific to the business process. All of this will be done with the direct interactive participation and contribution of your subject-matter experts.

---

[21] Discovery sessions – how they are conducted and with whom – will be discussed in detail in later.

As soon as possible after you've wrapped up a discovery session with subject-matter experts, and you have cleaned up all the resulting specifications and documentation – issue the business requirements dealing with the *business event* to all the stakeholders and SMEs who participated in your discovery session.

"As soon as possible" could be the same day, but is certainly within a day or two. The sooner it's done, the more responsive you'll be seen to be, and the more enthusiastic the response from your SMEs will be too.

Three things are important in this very agile and lean process.

First – your documentation for a single *business event* will be very small. Typically, you will be asking them to review just 3 or 4 pages. It will consist of two pages describing the process that supports the *business event*. The diagram will be on one page and the process narrative will be on the other page, if it doesn't fit under the diagram. For each of the Objects identified in the process diagram you will have a definition, data attributes and business rules. Since most diagrams only have 3 or 4 Objects, usually not more than six, this makes the documentation pretty lean. Send this to the subject-matter experts who participated in the discovery session. Ask them to read and review the document, particularly the business rules for the Objects, since these define the behavior of the new system. Give them a deadline for feedback or their approval that it represents what you discussed in the discovery session.

Second – what your SMEs receive will look exactly like the diagrams you drew in the actual discovery session, just a little prettier … so they will recognize what they are reviewing. Most of them will be very comfortable with this, since you have already spent some time on the business process and the business rules in the discovery session. Also, all the information contained in the very slim document is their knowledge, not yours. They will recognize it as such.

Third – your fast and timely distribution of the documentation means it's still fresh in their minds. As they read, they will recall what was discussed. This provides the continuity you need to get good feedback. It will also stimulate them to get the feedback to you as quickly as possible.

I have found this to be an exceptionally fast, agile and lean way of getting good feedback quickly, and a good way of keeping subject-matter experts involved past the very interactive discovery sessions. It's a way of overcoming the "out of sight, out of mind" syndrome, which can have so much effect on project progress.

So, what tools can you use for documentation?

Let's get one issue out of the way. I am opposed to the use of technical software (you know the kind) because every one of them is designed to help software engineers, not your business partners. What they see and what they get is totally alien to their business world.

In terms of what works well, the most commonly used is still simple documents, emailed internally. But a Project Wiki could be an excellent alternative; and I would recommend the use of an expert-moderated Wiki for any project.

A Project Wiki is particularly good for teams that are dispersed across the country, around the world, or even in different offices across the city. Feedback can be almost instant, and knowledge will be contributed by the people who have the knowledge.

A Project Wiki has two lives. The first is when it is the knowledge repository consisting of the business requirements specification preceding software installation. The second is its life after the software is implemented. The transition from a Business Requirement Wiki to a Project Wiki, with specific business area sub-domains, takes place when stakeholders and subject-matter experts start to maintain the knowledge contained in the business requirements as a knowledge set of the business areas. Since this includes all areas and interfaces, not just those features developed as software support. The Project Wiki, with specific business area sub-domains, becomes a teaching and learning tool for the affected business areas.

The intent of any Project Wiki is to make changes easy to do, not difficult. Traditional documentation is always difficult to maintain, and is never maintained very well, if at all.

When a Project Wiki is developed this way, maintenance of the business documentation now becomes the responsibility of the client and the SMEs in the different business areas.

The documentation you need, whether for a single *business event*, or all of them, is summarized on the following page.

The Business Requirements Document

Project Business Event List
(from the *Project Scope Blitz*)

- List of project *business events* from the *Project Scope Blitz*, including business area ownership and involvement, and requirement priority.

SALES AND PROCUREMENT PROJECT
AIR Telecom Inc.

List of Potential Events	SALES	MARKETING	PURCHASING	ACCOUNTING	Priority (1, 2, 3)
1 A Customer Buys a Product	★	★		★	1
2 A Customer Requests an Unavailable Product	★	★			1
3 A Product is Returned by a Customer	★	★		★	1
4 It is Time to Determine a Salesperson's Commissions	★			★	2
5 It is Time to Order a Product from a Supplier	★	★	★	★	1
6 It is Time to Pay a Supplier for Product Delivered	★	★	★	★	1

Total Number of Events = 6
Pilot & Copilot: Days to BRD = 2.7
Pilot Only: Days to BRD = 4.4

Fig. 5.9: Example of a Project Business Event List

For each Event (*n* occurrences)

- A **Business Process Diagram** that supports the *business event*.
- A task-based narrative for the Business process.
- References or links to Object definitions.
- A list of Business Areas affected by the Business process
- A Business Rules Table for Objects supporting the business process.
- Any Implementation (design solution) considerations.

For each Object (*n* occurrences)

- Definition of the Object.
- Business Rules for the Object.
- Data attributes for the Object.
- Primary (unique) identifier.

The Business Rules Table (BRT)

- Matrix of intersecting Objects.
- Cardinality (0,1,N) for each Object.

BRT	customer	product	payment
1 customer		1,N,0	1,N,0
1 product	1,N,0		1,N,0
1 payment	1	1,N	

Fig. 5.10: Example of a Business Rules Table

5.3 Are Composite Diagrams Still OK?

In one of my seminars, someone once said, *"I was taught to do several process diagrams together on a page – more or less seven – to integrate related processes for an area? Should I join some of these event-based process diagrams together to make composite diagrams?"*

No – normally, we don't. When using an event-based approach to analysis, such as PowerStart Business Analysis, we have not found any particular reason to do this, except that it was a necessity with the original 'structured analysis' methods. It was done that way because the data flow diagrams of 'structured analysis' resulted from how you approached progressive decomposition of higher level diagrams.

Let me suggest that you ask the <u>Inclusion Question</u> to deal with this issue: *"If we join the process diagrams together, what will this enable us to do that we couldn't do if they were not joined together?"* … or, as an <u>Exclusion Question</u>, *"If we don't join the process diagrams together, what will this prevent us from doing that we must be able to do?"*

The usual answer is, *"We need a composite diagram so we can get the bigger picture."*

Well, that's interesting, but what do we mean by "the bigger picture"?

What are we really looking for here? And how will we recognize it when we see it? My understanding is that "the bigger picture" is an issue left over from another way of doing things in earlier years. Almost all older systems were serial and procedural in nature; therefore, it was very important to see how things were connected and how data moved from one process to another. The systems of yesterday were generally monoliths, with almost everything happening as serial progression. Most communication was by way of data flows rather than through Objects and their data.

Today, we know that it's not necessary to take this same serial approach. Instead, we can take an approach based on *business events*. A set of *business events* is really just a set of circumstances that a system has to deal with, not serial in nature, and all the supporting data is Object based.

So, how do we see "the bigger picture"? Well, it depends on what someone needs to know about the so-called "bigger picture".

If we want to see how we can <u>access information,</u> we can extract a prescription for database design[22] by generating a conceptual data model from the **Business Rules Table**.

The Conceptual Data Model, created by database designers, is one view of the "bigger picture" – as a composite diagram – and tells the software engineers how Objects of related information are logically joined, and how to get from one Object to another to find related information.

BRT		Salesperson	Customer	Outlet
1	Salesperson		N, 0	1, N
1	Customer	1, N, 0		1, N
1	Outlet	N	N	

Partial Conceptual Data Model

Fig. 5.11: Business Rules Table with corresponding Chen ER diagram

In the example above, the notation in the **Business Rules Table** converts easily into a partial conceptual data model diagram. The only things that remain to be done are to resolve the many-to-many relationships between Objects (an easy process), and complete the data attribution to Objects.

Do individual diagrams need to be joined together into a series of composite diagrams? I don't think so.[23] In all the projects I have ever worked on, using this event-based approach to business requirements analysis, I have never found the need. But if it makes you feel better to do it, there's no real harm in it. Be forewarned, however, that it takes a lot longer (because there's extra work to do), and I would suggest there is no benefit in the exercise. If you can't identify the reason for the need, don't do it.

---

[22] A "prescription" for database design is not a solution design. It is simply a specification that states, "these are the data relationships and accesses you need to be able to build a database solution" to meet the data access requirements specified by the business.

[23] Although joining some of these business processes together when developing a <u>solution design</u> is another matter.

Chapter 6. The Discovery Sessions –
How to Involve Your Subject-Matter Experts

Contents

A 'requirements discovery session' is an interactive approach to conducting meetings with clients and subject-matter experts to probe and establish a project's business or organizational requirements. These highly interactive sessions include clients, business partners, subject-matter experts, business analysts, executives and some system professionals. These discovery sessions are based on the sound principles of JAD[24], but with greater flexibility and more suited to the 21st century. Discovery sessions are even faster than conventional RAD[25] sessions.

Requirements discovery sessions produce great savings by shortening the elapsed time required to gather business system requirements and by improving the completeness and quality of the requirements gathered. This reduces significantly the number of costly downstream requirements changes. Requirements discovery sessions have been extremely successful with many organizations worldwide, private and government alike. However, the success of a requirements discovery session is not just a function of the business analysis methodology you use, it requires a well-practiced professional to lead the sessions (a senior practitioner) and the unreserved participation of clients, business partners, subject-matter experts and executives. In other words, there must be a real commitment by the organization's client base, not just words of

---

[24] Joint Application Development or Joint Application Design (JAD) was developed by Chuck Morris of IBM Raleigh (North Carolina) and Tony Crawford of IBM Toronto (Canada) in the late 1970's. In 1980 Crawford and Morris taught JAD in Toronto and Crawford led several workshops to prove the concept. The results were encouraging and JAD became a well-accepted approach in many companies. In time, JAD developed and gained general industry approval as a best practice. Crawford defines JAD as an interactive systems design concept involving discussion groups in a workshop setting. Originally, JAD was designed to bring system developers and users of varying backgrounds and opinions together in a productive and creative environment. The meetings were a way of obtaining system requirements and specifications.

[25] Rapid Application Development (RAD) is based on JAD, but moves along faster by applying the 80/20 Rule in development and scope selectivity.

support. "Real commitment" means putting in the time necessary to participate in discovery sessions – which is a lot less than the time required by conventional analysis methods.

There are two kinds of requirements discovery sessions: the *Project Scope Blitz* and the detailed discovery session.

6.1 The Risks and Rewards of Discovery Sessions

There are two major risks when planning requirements discovery sessions. Whether the discovery session is intended to be a front-end *Project Scope Blitz* or a series of regular detailed discovery sessions, there are often unrealistic productivity expectations (a) before the discovery session, and (b) after discovery sessions.

Also, when an organization embarks on a series of discovery sessions without being fully committed to the highly interactive nature of these sessions, it can fail or fall short of the mark. But if an organization devotes the right amount of time and the right people, the results will be substantial. Some of the benefits of a requirements discovery session include:

- It accelerates the business revitalization and process re-engineering exercise.

- It accelerates the business requirements learning process.

- It massively increases productivity by shortening the iteration cycle.

- It ensures the highest quality possible, because of direct participation by clients and subject-matter experts.

- It ensures the most complete business requirements analysis in the shortest period of time.

- It helps to develop mutual respect between consultants and clients.

- It provides a forum for exploring focused, in-context business revitalization ideas.

- It helps to deliver what the client needs and wants, quickly.

- It opens the door to success.

How the requirements discovery session is conducted is what sets it apart from other approaches to gathering business requirements. Critical ingredients for a successful discovery session include leadership from a trained and experienced practitioner and an expert scribe (also a business specialist); as well as participation by executive sponsors, key decision makers and *real* subject-matter experts[26]; and the ability to work without the usual daily interruptions[27].

6.2 What is a Requirements Discovery Session?

The Project Scope Blitz.

The objectives of a *Project Scope Blitz* are as follows:

- To quickly identify many of the *business events* that will be part of the target system.

- To determine the business areas or departments that have responsibility for responding to and dealing with the identified *business events*.

- To accurately predict the amount of time required to complete the detailed discovery sessions with clients and SMEs, and to prepare the **Business Requirements Document**.

- To establish work priorities – which *business events* will be done first, and which ones will be done later.

- To enable planning of the schedule for detailed discovery sessions with clients and subject-matter experts.

- To determine the effort and cost of the project's business system requirements analysis.

Detailed Discovery Sessions.

The objectives of a detailed discovery session are as follows:

- To quickly get all subject-matter experts on the same page, at the same time.

- To quickly uncover and discover the project's business requirements for one or more *business events* in a single session with one or more subject-matter experts.

---

[26] A real subject-matter expert has in-depth practical knowledge of the business areas affected by the project, and their work processes. This person also understands why work processes are organized the way they are, and what these processes are to achieve. This is not a surrogate user; nor is it a recent business school graduate who can fill the gap.

[27] Discovery sessions can last anywhere from an hour to several days, depending on the critical nature of the project. Discovery sessions should be uninterrupted, as much as possible, since the absence of key people delays progress.

- To enable the business system analyst to focus on a small component (a *business event*) and to quickly learn about the business requirements in support of that *business event*.

- To discover complete and accurate business requirements, focused and in context – not just "goodness and light".

- To achieve "buy-in" and ownership from clients and subject-matter experts.

- To develop mutual respect by all participants – subject-matter experts and business system analysts.

How long does a Discovery session take?

The Project Scope Blitz.

Project Scope Blitz sessions take about a half-day, sometimes a little more. For an average project, if the client has a good handle on their business needs, a half-day session is often enough.

It's important before planning the regular detailed discovery sessions for a project to estimate how many *business events* there will be and how much time is needed for each one. You also need to know who should participate – clients and subject-matter experts.

SALES AND PROCUREMENT PROJECT
AIR Telecom Inc.

	List of Potential Events	SALES	MARKETING	PURCHASING	ACCOUNTING	Priority (1, 2, 3)
1	A Customer Buys a Product	★	★		★	1
2	A Customer Requests an Unavailable Product	★	★			1
3	A Product is Returned by a Customer	★	★		★	1
4	It is Time to Determine a Salesperson's Commissions	★			★	2
5	It is Time to Order a Product from a Supplier	★	★	★	★	1
6	It is Time to Pay a Supplier for Product Delivered	★	★	★	★	1

Total Number of Events = 6
Pilot & Copilot: Days to BRD = 2.7
Pilot Only: Days to BRD = 4.4

Fig. 6.1: A short Project Business Event List

The *Project Scope Blitz* is very interactive with clients and subject-matter experts. It involves extracting from them the things they believe should be within the scope of the project. Our experience is that the more senior the participants are, the better your results will be.

Before continuing, please review the earlier section on *business events*, Chapter 1: The Business Event. You will recall that a *business event* is a situation, condition, circumstance or external requirement. It is not a process. The process is <u>what</u> we do to supports the *business event* – not <u>how</u>.

When you start up a *Project Scope Blitz*, you can start by asking the participants about some of the things they need to have in their business system. Their answers will not be in the form of *business events*. It's up to you, as the consultant-analyst, to distill what they say and turn it into a *business event* statement. When you do hear what they say, and you turn it into a *business event* statement, it is best to confirm with the speaker if your understanding of their requirement, as you have stated it in your *business event* statement, is correct.

Each time you identify a *business event*, it must be listed and displayed so the participants can see what you are doing, and they can read the *business event* statement as you have written it. My preferred method is to write the *business events* statements with a marker pen on *Write On – Cling On Sheets*[28] which stick to the wall.

You can also use higher technology, involving a projector. As *business event* statements are captured in a document, they can be projected onto a wall for everyone to see. The important point is, everyone gets to see what's being documented. In this way, they can see what you hear.

One approach that we recommend when conducting a *Project Scope Blitz*, is to create a short list of *business events* yourself, and then present these as "potential events" to your clients and subject-matter experts – one at a time. It's very important to suggest them strictly as "potential events" since participants are more likely to buy-in to their own knowledge and contributions than to yours. This approach is particularly useful if you don't have much information about the project, or when the project deals with something that's new or different.

The whole idea behind this use of "potential events" is to stimulate participation by the clients and subject-matter experts that are part of your *Project Scope Blitz*. In the early part of any interactive session, people are often hesitant to say anything or to get the ball rolling. If this is the case, then it's easy for you to toss out a "potential event" and to ask participants if that *business event* is something that could be part of the scope of the project. The answer could be a blunt *"no"*, in which case you strike it from your list.

---

[28] Since not everyone has a Smart Board, *Write On – Cling On Sheets*™ are white poly static sheets that come in about 3-foot squares that stick to walls – and anything else – and act like a whiteboard. You can erase what you write or draw on them with a marker, and you can move the sheets around, or roll them up. They can also be reused. A Google search will find this product for you.

Hopefully, it will stimulate discussion and determine if a "potential event" is a real *business event*, in scope or not.

After completing a *Project Scope Blitz*, you will have a long or short list of *business events* for the project. There's no doubt you will <u>not</u> have discovered all of the required *business events*, but you will have enough to get you started.

For each *business event* in the project, you will need to plan one detailed discovery session. Your plan should provide for four (4) hours per *business event* to complete all the documentation; but the detailed discovery session itself should only have one (1) hour per *business event* of discovery time with clients and subject-matter experts, regardless of its perceived complexity or simplicity.

Detailed Discovery Sessions.

A regular detailed discovery session for one *business event* should be scheduled for one (1) hour with clients and subject-matter experts.

An "average" project, we have found, is between 25-75 *business events*; "small" is less than 25 *business events*; and "large" is over 75 *business events*. Based on needing one hour of discovery time per *business event*, a "small" project needs less than 25 hours of client and SME time; an "average" project needs between 25 and 75 hours of client and SME time; and a "large" project needs over 75 hours of their time.

If necessary, this can all be scheduled one hour at a time, over an extended period.

For mission critical projects, detailed discovery sessions for a project can also be scheduled, one hour per *business event*, on consecutive days with all parties involved. This "complete immersion" approach is very effective (arguably the most effective approach), but also very exhausting for subject-matter experts and for the consultant. We must also consider that clients and SMEs have their own work to do, and dedicating several full days to discovery sessions is usually difficult.

Regardless of the approach you take – and I do recommend the scheduling of one-hour sessions – each *business event* needs an average of three (3) additional hours by the consultant to dig up more details with SMEs, apply Business Data Rule # 5 to extract new Objects (see section 2.4, page 48: Business Data Rule # 5) and add them to the **Business Rules Table**, convene meetings with SMEs to determine the rules that come from the new Objects, perhaps convene additional detailed discovery sessions for *business events* that are found from the new Objects and rules; and, complete the documentation.

The detailed discovery session is a team activity, therefore typical teamwork guidelines apply. It usually takes a project team, consisting of analysts and SMEs, a couple of days of detailed discovery sessions to jell and to ramp up on foundation information.

What kind of Facility is Required?

Any room with lots of uncluttered wall space will do. The wall space is important so you can put *Write On – Cling On Sheets* on them to draw the diagrams you need, so everyone who is in the room can see what has been done.

While there is lots of technology that can project the diagrams onto a screen or a wall, including Smart Boards, we have found the dynamics and comfort level of participants when using *Write On – Cling On* sheets and whiteboards can't be duplicated.

Participants should be seated comfortably with desk or table space.

Who should Participate?

A detailed discovery session should include a number of key people. Each discovery session should include clients and subject-matter experts who are crucial to the success of the project, including senior managers, other business partners with a stake in the project, project 'primes' and any other persons who have a good understanding of the project's objectives, business rationale, and re-engineering vision.

A business and its systems can only be as good as the dedication and participation shown by its owners and stakeholders. All participants in a detailed discovery session must bring an open mind. These discovery sessions enable participants to "liberate the mind" and potentially discover business re-engineering opportunities, including immediate opportunities for improvement[29]. These IOIs, often uncovered in discovery sessions, can be invaluable to an agile organization.

Participants in detailed discovery sessions should include the following:

Discovery Session Leader – The Pilot.

The "Pilot" is a consultant – a business system analyst – who leads and facilitates discovery sessions. We use the term "Pilot" because he or she must lead the session, keep it on course, and take it to its desired destination without problems.

---

[29] An 'Immediate Opportunity for Improvement', or 'IOI', is an opportunity discovered during requirements analysis that can be acted upon almost immediately and can lead to substantial business process improvement and added value to the business.

Without a doubt, the "Pilot" is most instrumental to the success of the detailed discovery session, and the successful "Pilot" has an exceptional combination of skills.

- The "Pilot" must have excellent communication and cooperation skills – a skilled servant leader.

- The "Pilot" must be able to deal with political disputes, power struggles and personality clashes, although this doesn't happen very often.

- The "Pilot" needs to be completely impartial, with no political baggage, and able to keep an open mind while managing conversations.

- The "Pilot" must be sensitive to hidden agendas and be able to redirect them constructively.

- The "Pilot" must be able to bridge communication gaps – technical, linguistic and cultural.

- The "Pilot" must be comfortable speaking to and managing a group of people that often includes senior executives.

- The "Pilot" must encourage quiet group members to contribute their thoughts, and manage positively strong personalities that sometimes dominate sessions.

Achieving all of this is not for the faint-of-heart. Therefore, the "Pilot" must have the respect of those who participate in discovery sessions. That respect is earned through a series of successful discovery sessions, but it also comes from general comportment, dress, civility, respect for participants, and being non-judgmental of contributions.

Our experience is that when a requirements discovery session fails, it is almost always because of the session leader or facilitator.

One of the reasons for session failure is when an organization wants to train several people as "Pilots", but they lack sufficient recognition of the value of experience. Some managers (thankfully, not too many) believe they can assign a new "Pilot" to a project immediately after a candidate has finished an analysis course. Unfortunately, the result of trying to get everyone up to speed immediately, without the blessings and pain of experience, is that almost no one gets there. This, in turn, can lead to unskilled "Pilots" and weak results. Weak results can lead to backsliding to the endless search for an analysis methodology "that works". Of course, the methodology works just fine; problems are usually the result of "Pilot" error.

It is my opinion that an organization that intends to use this approach – PowerStart Business Analysis – as an effective way of eliciting and gathering business requirements should train, and support, a small core group of expert

"Pilot" practitioners. These "Pilots" should conduct as many discovery sessions throughout the year as possible. Our experience is that it takes about four projects for a new "Pilot" to become reasonably proficient. And it quickly gets better after that.

Expert Scribe – The Co-Pilot.

The "co-pilot" must truly be *expert*. The "co-pilot" can't just be the next available body. They must be fully trained in business requirements analysis and how a discovery session is run. They must know what they are hearing when they hear it; such as Objects, data attributes and business rules. And they must have the knowledge and ability to back up the "Pilot", if required. We call this person a 'co-pilot' for just that reason.

The primary role of the "co-pilot" is to record what is said and done in the detailed discovery session. As such, this person will actively participate to make sure everything that's said and done is clear and concise.

Sometimes a "Pilot" is their own "co-pilot"; i.e., they wear a different hat at different times. However, if a "Pilot" is supported by someone else as "co-pilot", the time it takes to complete all the requirements documentation for the project is about half of what's needed if the "Pilot" works alone as both "Pilot" and "co-pilot".

An Expert Coach.

For the first four projects we recommend that consultant/analyst be supported by an expert coach: Someone who is expert at this approach to business systems analysis. Having a coach who is experienced with this approach will lead to mastery of the methods and project success much faster, and with fewer challenges. This is a common practice in almost all professions and trades. It is time that we assured our own success by applying this best practice.

Executive Sponsors and Project Primes.

If you want the project to succeed, make sure an executive sponsor or a fully empowered project prime participate in the *Project Scope Blitz*. The absence of these people sends the message that the project isn't important enough for participation by other business partners and subject-matter experts.

Subject-Matter Experts and other Business Partners.

Get them involved as much as possible and as quickly as possible. Involve the client directly, as well as the subject-matter experts. Involve as many of the key people from the affected business areas and department as quickly as you can. They should have a deep interest and enthusiasm for the success of the project. They should be the decision-makers, as well as the subject-matter experts (and these may be the same people). Their knowledge of the business and their vision is instrumental to the success of the sessions.

6.3 Key Success Factors

There are many success factors that are unique to each particular discovery session. However, there are some generally accepted success factors that apply to just about any kind of interactive session:

- Be sure that the project's executive sponsors and key stakeholders attend and actively participate in the initial *Project Scope Blitz*.

- Issue the **Project Business Event List** to everyone who participated in the *Project Scope Blitz* as soon as possible after the session is done. It should go out no later than a day after the session.

- Set realistic expectations for the work to be done in the detailed discovery sessions, and a realistic schedule. In terms of the time required, plan on one (1) hour per *business event*, with clients and SMEs participating, and an additional three (3) hours per *business events* to complete the analysis and documentation. That will be fast, and realistic.[30] Also, never plan on more than five hours of productive work per day for any member of your team.

- Be very visible by conducting discovery sessions with all the people required to be involved in a *business event*. Avoid one-person interviews. They are inefficient, take much too long, and hide your visibility. Visibility demonstrates that you are not only gathering the requirements, but you are *seen* to be gathering the requirements.

- If the project becomes a software acquisition or development project, make sure the software engineers (the programmers, database designers and system designers) know how to read the **Business Requirements Document** and, if custom building the software, how to turn it into a solution design.

- Do a lot of discovery sessions, every chance you get; but perfect practice – with a coach and mentor for "Pilots" and "co-pilots" – works better than practice without guidance by an expert. Having a coach experienced in this kind of business system analysis will lead to mastery of the methods much faster, and project success with fewer challenges.

Other general success factors include:

- Actively encourage everyone to participate. Instead of being just a facilitator, be a proactive "Pilot" and leader. This is what a real consultant does.

- Have well established and agreed upon objectives for each discovery session. Explain to participants how a discovery session will generally only deal with

---

[30] You may not actually need the additional three hours for every *business event*. For some, you'll be able to clean it up and get it ready for distribution in less than 30 minutes, but for others it could take 6 or even 12 hours, depending on what you discover in your post-discovery session assessment. The three hours is an average over all the *events*. Therefore, if you have 30 events, you'll need 30 one-hour discovery sessions with SMEs, and 90 additional hours of finishing work.

the *business event* scheduled and the business process, Objects, data, and business rules needed to support it. Explain how you may find new, previously undiscovered *business events*, but these will not be dealt with in the current discovery session. New *events* discovered will be added to the **Project Business Event (Parking Lot)** and will be done at some later time in the schedule. You will probably have to revise or extend the schedule; but that's not new either, and it's perfectly normal.

- Be unbiased and neutral about the business requirement. As a consultant it is your responsibility to determine what the client needs to support the business. It is not your job to assess the correctness or value of the client's requirements. While you may suggest a path (by using questions rather than answers), it is the client's responsibility to identify the business processes and data that add value to the business.

- "Keep it as simple as possible, but no simpler."[31]

- Keep focused on the objectives – stay with the subject *business event*, and don't jump to other unplanned subjects. Use the **Project Business Event List (Parking Lot)** for other *business events* that come up in discussion, or as a result of querying the **Business Rules Table**.

- Lead the discovery process … facilitate the requirements. Be the servant leader that every consultant must be.

- Complete the **Business Rules Table**, and its questions, immediately after finishing the **Business-Process Diagram** that supports a *business event*.

- Use the client's terminology – no technobabble.

- Don't judge the client's questions and answers. If you didn't understand what they said, or if it just sounded strange, ask them to help you understand their question or answer.

- Never fear that your questions will sound strange or uninformed. I've found that this is actually a good thing, even when I have to pretend to understand less than I actually do. People love to tell you about what they do and their responsibilities. They also love to tell you what they know. And that's what discovery sessions are all about – getting the expert knowledge from the subject-matter experts.

- Challenge the SME's thinking, not the SME. Sounds good, but how do you do that? The first step is to never ask *"Why?"* when they give you an answer. "Why?" is not a good question to ask adults. It in effect asks them to justify or rationalize their answer, and they are not there to do that. If a senior sales manager says, *"We want a report on widgets sold in the northwest region"*, and you're not quite certain what this means, it's not a good idea to ask that manager *"Why?"* The answer you get is probably not what you're looking for. Instead, replace your desire to ask "Why?" with the following question:

---

[31] With thanks to Albert Einstein.

"John, if we have the report on widget sales in the northwest region, what will that enable us to do that we have to be able to do?" … or, from another perspective, *"John, if we don't have the report on widget sales in the northwest region, what will that prevent us from doing that we must be able to do?"* You'll get a real answer with either of these questions (which are just two sides of the same coin). The answer you get will be the real *business event* that you're looking for.

- Be clear and understandable. Don't mumble. Use complete sentences consisting of both nouns and verbs, at least most of the time. Don't use techno-babble or terms the subject-matter experts are not familiar with. Avoid using acronyms unless they are common to your industry (which means many others besides yourself must know the acronym).

- Make people feel good. The better they feel, the more readily they will participate in future discovery sessions. Be good finding.

- Smile. A lot. People respond a whole lot better to smiles, especially if the subject is serious and sometimes complicated.

- Have fun. Use your good sense of humor. If this is sometimes difficult for you, work on developing a sense of humor.

- Listen… listen… and listen some more. What people say and what they mean are sometimes a little different. Keep really focused on what they mean. When you're not sure, ask them to *"help me understand that better"*.

- If you are asked a question, you must <u>always</u> respond to the participant's answer in some manner.

These are some of the key success factors. Undoubtedly, there are many others that apply equally well.

6.4 Tips and Techniques for Discovery Sessions

About The Discovery Sessions

- When starting a requirements discovery session, remember to ground the participants in the fact that you will be focusing on the **'WHAT'**, not the **'HOW'**. Keep reminding them of this if they drift into how things should be done (solution design) or other solution discussions.

- Remember the basic principle of *"Partition the effort to minimize complexity"*. If the business process is becoming too complex, it's probably because the subject-matter experts are attempting to have one process support several *business events*. While this is natural, try to keep it as simple as possible. Simple works. Don't try to make it more complex. Go with it until you know better. Don't speculate about what you don't know.

- Optics is important in discovery sessions. Print legibly on the whiteboards or *Write On – Cling On Sheets*, and use **red** and **blue** as alternating colors when going through the process. It helps visual recognition of material for your subject-matter experts, the "co-pilot", and you, the "Pilot". Stay away from the other colors, since most of them can't be seen very well from even a few feet away.

- At the completion of each **Business Process Diagram**, walk through (or talk through) the process as a wrap-up, so your SMEs can confirm its substance once again. It also enables your "co-pilot" to validate that the narrative has been recorded accurately.

- As the "Pilot", periodically check to ensure that the "co-pilot" is keeping up to you. Before a detailed discovery session, work out signals between the two of you so the "co-pilot" can indicate a need to catch up before moving forward.

- As the "Pilot", listen for the "co-pilot's" fingers hitting the keyboard. If there is dead silence, take a break from the discovery session and speak with your "co-pilot" to determine if everything is OK – that the "co-pilot" is actually capturing the information as it arises during the discovery session. Also listen for the pace of keying; i.e., is the "co-pilot" still keying something while you are ready to move ahead to the next topic. Or, has keying stopped and it appears the "co-pilot" is also ready to move on. This is particularly an issue when going through the 'BRT Questions' in the **Business Rules Table**.

- Tracking requirements in a system can be done by identifying attributes in Objects that define a particular status (e.g., open, closed, approved, rejected, etc.). Attributing a *date/time* data item to each different status will provide a complete record of an instance of an Object as it changes state in a system.

- Remember that an "inventory" is really a list of many instances of a particular Object, each having its own unique identifier (key). If you are looking at inventory management *business events*, consider having a status attribute on the Object (e.g., sold, available, returned, etc.) with an associated *date/time*. This will easily provide the information needed to create reports, issue product reorders, etc.

About The Business Process Diagrams

- A data flow line that goes <u>from</u> an Object <u>into</u> a **Business Process Diagram** represents **finding** information (data items) about that source Object in order to satisfy the requirements of a task in the process.

Fig. 6.2: Data flow as input to a process

- A data flow line that goes <u>into</u> an Object <u>from</u> the process represents **recording** or **remembering** information (data items) about that Object. This satisfies the requirement in the process to update or record changes to individual data items, or to create a new instance of an Object.

Fig. 6.3: Data flow as output from a process

- Avoid using the words "update" and "modify" on data flow dialogues. Use pointier words like "**record**" and "**remember**". If you need to add extra emphasis to the data flow, you can also identify the name of the data item in the data dialogue.

- A double-headed arrow between the process and an Object (i.e., an arrow on each end) represents a 'Query/Response' task action – a dialogue. This is nothing more than personal style and preference.

Fig. 6.4: A dialogue data flow

- Always ensure that the name of the *business event* that's the subject of the **Business Process Diagram** is identified on the top of the diagram. If you find the conversation with your SMEs drifting, point to the *business event* name with the question, "*Is this conversation about this business event, or another one?*" This refocuses the discussion, and may even lead to the identification of a new *business event* that was missing from the original list.

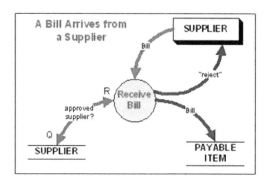

Fig. 6.5: Always identify 'event statement' at top of a process diagram

- A business process does <u>not</u> always have a **Terminator** as a 'stimulus' to start the process, or end it. Stimuli for initiating the process can come from an Object (e.g., a data attribute), or can be a specific time or date that kicks off the process.

About The Objects

- Following the 5 Business Data Rules (section 2.4, page 51: Summary of the Business Data Rules) is extremely important for clarity of the finished business requirements. In particular, watch out for multi-valued data items ('mv') as they may indicate the need to create a new Object that is 'characteristic' of the original Object.

- Always remember to get your SMEs to provide a concise definition of an Object. It ensures everyone has the same understanding of what the Object represents. Interestingly, Object definitions expand considerably during most detailed discovery sessions, so don't be happy with the first definition you encounter. It will probably change as you progress with the discovery sessions.

- Always think of Objects in the singular. It helps ground people in understanding the purpose of the business process without getting distracted by number of instances, time, etc. Also, we (people) are not very good at thinking through multiplicity. Stick to the singular.

- Always name an Object in the singular, even though it represents all possible occurrences of the Object, including its history. Your diagrams represent the business view of the information, not a database design view.

- If a multi-valued ("mv") data item is identified in an Object, but there is no immediate need during a discovery session to break it out into its own

Object, do so after the discovery session if it improves the detail of the analysis. If this results in a new Object, you will have to revisit the questions it will generate through the **Business Rules Table**, and the answers it will produce.

About The Business Rules Table

- When writing the business rules that come from the **Business Rules Table** and form part of an Object, is important to ensure that a descriptive verb is used to express the business rule properly. It is likely that you can use the verb you used to name the **Business Process Diagram**, but this doesn't always work. Try to choose a verb structure that represents the context of the **Business Process Diagram**. In a worst-case scenario, when you just can't figure out the right verb structure, use 'have' or 'be' as a standby.

- Sometimes, the answer to the first placeholder 'BRT Questions' is, *"We don't really care"* or *"We don't have an interest in that"*. In this case, put an "N/A" (not applicable) in the intersection cell of the two Objects that were queried. The fact that there may not be any interest in a specific anchor Object having a relationship with another specific Object in the circumstance identified (the *business event* you're working on), does not mean there won't be an interest in them under another circumstance.

About The 'Co-Pilot"

The "co-pilot" is as important to the success of the discovery session as the "Pilot". They have different but equally important roles. The following notes are for "co-pilots" who work with "Pilots" by documenting everything as it happens during a detailed discovery session.[32]

During the Discovery Session

- **Have the "Pilot" explain your role as "co-pilot".**

  Initially, as a "co-pilot", people will wonder why you are there and what you are recording. Will their words be held against them? Are you a spy? Clarify that you are there to ensure that the information discovered during this session is appropriately documented. Let participants know that a **Business Requirements Document** will be produced as soon as possible after all the discovery sessions are done. If the **Business Requirements Document**, or some part of it will be distributed, let them know that too.

- **Listen, listen, and listen some more.**

  Often, there will be more than one conversation taking place. The challenge is to figure out which is the key one. Try to stay focused on the same dialogue

---

[32] Not all projects have both a Pilot and Co-pilot. Some projects have a Pilot only, who also fills the role of Co-pilot. This would be one of those famous "team of one" projects.

as the "Pilot" is engaged in. Because the "Pilot" will likely be actively listening to a specific discussion, encourage others to speak up (at the right time) if you are aware of other side discussions taking place.

- **Seek clarification.**

  If there is something you don't understand, ask for clarification. Most people in the room don't expect you to be an expert in the business at hand – that's their job. Your role is to ensure that the facts, as well as the thoughts and concerns of the SMEs get appropriately documented. Consequently, if you do not understand, or if the discussion has gone off in several directions, it is absolutely appropriate to ask participants to repeat their words to ensure that the discussion is accurately documented.

  However, as the expert "co-pilot", there is an expectation that you will have some innate ability to hear all, understand all, and document all. Sometimes you may find that it is more appropriate to follow up with specific individuals off line. Your good judgment is necessary.

- **Read back complex narratives or business rules for confirmation.**

  If a particularly complex business process has been under discussion for some time, it may be appropriate to request a break so that you can consolidate your notes. If you do, after the break read back the updated version of the narrative or the business rules.

- **Define all acronyms.**

  If acronyms are used in the discovery session (and they almost always are), make a note of them and follow up with individuals off line to ensure complete understanding. Ensure that full definitions of these terms are included at least once in the document. If appropriate, consider adding a glossary of acronyms as an appendix.

- **If participants wish to see what you're doing, share it with them on breaks.**

  Remember, the document you are preparing belongs to everyone in the room. It is the consolidation of all their thoughts, ideas and experience. If they want to grab a glimpse on a break, share it with them. This is an excellent opportunity to check with individuals one-on-one to validate specific comments in the document. This will also enhance their confidence that their words are being recorded appropriately and that a great deal of work is being done by you, the scribing "co-pilot", as well as by the people in the room.

- **Leave the diagrams for later.**

  A **Business Process Diagram** will likely change as you progress through the discovery session. The diagrams are usually on *Write On – Cling On Sheets* on the wall. Use the diagrams to get the process narratives correct during the session. Once the process definition and diagram are stable, add the diagram to your documentation.

Outside the Discovery Session

- **Add the diagrams to your documentation.**

  Copy the diagrams from the whiteboards or *Write on – Cling On Sheets* on the walls to your documentation during the consolidation period at the end of the day, when there are no clients or subject-matter experts around. Since diagrams can change during a discovery session as you get more information, there will be no time for you to capture the diagrams (perhaps more than once) during the session.

- **Create a backup of the diagrams.**

  Before you move any of the diagrams on *Write On – Cling On Sheets*, create backup copies by using your trusty digital camera or iPhone. Take photos of all the diagrams. For any specific **Business Process Diagram**, you may want to take more than one photo, as it can change as a result of discoveries in different sessions.

- **Confirm the content.**
  - Do the narratives make sense?
  - Do the definitions (Objects and data) make sense?
  - Do the relationships defined in the business rules make sense?
  - Do you have at least one example for every "*never*" answer from the 'BRT Questions'?
  - Have you checked all Objects in the Object-Task Table?

Other considerations

- Where appropriate, give key subject-matter experts an opportunity to "see" an early version of the documentation for a specific **Business Process Diagram** (which may support one or more *business events*). This gives them a sense of how much work is actually getting done. Visibility is one of the keys to success.

- When reviewing specific documentation with a subject-matter expert, be prepared for some "wordsmithing". This is why you are reviewing it – to ensure that the way the information is documented is how they want it. "Wordsmithing" is a step in the ownership process.

- As discussed earlier, consider posting individual processes and their supporting information as part of an internal Project Wiki. The business processes should represent what the organization wants, without detailing how it will be delivered, and it should be a living document. As a Project Wiki, with business area sub-domains, it can be used by the client community as a teaching or training tool, and it can easily be maintained by the client community that owns the business processes.

Tips and Techniques for Co-Pilots

Listening

During the detailed discovery session, concentrate on listening to what is being said. Business Process Diagrams and Object data attributes can be captured at the end of the day – they'll still be on the *Write On – Cling On Sheets* when all the subject-matter experts have left. Also, most narratives can be constructed from a good diagram quite easily. Look to the data flows to find the tasks.

There is a lot said during the Discovery Session by the Pilot and by the SMEs themselves that will not appear on any diagram you create, but needs to be captured in your narratives. Concentrate on combining what you see on your diagrams with what you've heard, and you should be able to build a process narrative that accurately describes the process taking place.

Judgment

A large part of being an expert Pilot or co-pilot is being able to determine what needs to be captured, and to distinguish the needed data from other information that arises during the discussion. Many times in a discovery session a SME will get caught up in an explanation that contains a lot of information which is not really applicable to the immediate work you are doing. You are not there to capture full descriptions of the job functions of everybody in the room. You only want to capture information that belongs to the project's business requirements. Any extraneous information captured means there is that much more for the readers of the document to wade through to get to the real requirements. And that's not a good thing.

However, you simply can't cut somebody off and tell them that the information they are providing, while it might be important, is not useful in the document. Use common sense, and be flexible. Sometimes, letting someone get off-track in an area they believe to be important, can actually be very productive. Listening is a proactive skill that also requires the good judgment to let someone be heard, even when there's not much direct value added.

Verification

Don't be afraid to interrupt, stop the discussion, and insure that what you've captured is what has been said. The information that you are capturing must represent what was said – you are building the definitive record of the business requirements. If you're not sure, double-check with the people that know best – the subject-matter experts.

If you're the co-pilot (and you're not part of that magical team-of-one when you're also the Pilot), be sure to discuss your 'interruption option' with the Pilot before the discovery session starts. Agree on the best way to verify your information where required, and try to stick to that method. Don't step on any toes. However, do not interrupt the discussion to add your own two cents worth regarding the business process. As the co-pilot you are not one of the subject-matter experts – that's why they are in the room.

If you have a vested interest in the outcome of the session, do not agree to be the co-pilot. If you're talking, you can't be listening or recording, and you'll very quickly find that you're falling behind in the capture of information. Your writing will also be biased, even if it is unintentional.

Teamwork

If you're the co-pilot, you and the Pilot are a team. Do your best to use your knowledge of business system analysis to know the direction in which the discussion could be heading, so you're not caught by surprise. Be ready to read back anything you've captured, at any time.

As a co-pilot, if you have any questions about what is drawn or annotated on a *Write On – Cling On Sheet*, ask the Pilot right away.

Technical Details

The business requirements concern the "what" and not the "how". It is not a technical specification. It is a business specification. That being said, there are times during discovery sessions when there are things mentioned that might not be considered to be business requirements, but might be information that's needed to populate the database once it is complete.

For example, let's say you're discussing gas tanks. A data Object called **GAS TANK** would have attributes such as *height, width, depth, location, weight, date entered into inventory,* and *capacity*. One of the SMEs might say, *"Well, none of our tanks can hold more than 100 gallons. Ever."* Although this is a piece of technical data (which is certainly implementation dependent, since it could change in the future), it could save some time at a later point in the project if this fact is noted now, and it won't take long to record it as part of the business requirements. The way to get around the "physical" nature of this data is to just enter it as a note in the description of the data attribute (*capacity*, in this example).

Five Phrases

For the purpose of writing narratives for business processes, here are five phrases I have found invaluable to kick-start the building of a process narrative.

1. "For each ..."
2. "Periodically ..."
3. "Determine ..."
4. "Remember (or record) ..."
5. "Find (or identify) ..."

Don't limit yourself to these particular phrases when building your narratives, but they may come in very handy if you find you can't think of how to word what you've just heard.

In addition to the word "Find" another word that might be helpful is "Identify". For example, when making a sale you want to remember who made the sale, but you don't need any sales person information and you don't need to record anything about the salesperson, except who they are. In this case, you might simply write, "Identify the **SALESPERSON** who made the sale."

The real key to being a successful expert "co-pilot" is to practice what you've learned. You'll find that the more you scribe, the better you'll be, and the easier it is to hear everything that's being said. You might even find, with lots of practice, that you can listen to two (or even three) conversations at the same time and pick out what's important in each of them. (Ideally, there should only ever be one conversation taking place in the room at the same time, but we all know that this isn't reality.)

Lastly, know the methodology you're learning. Not just learn it, but know it. Internalize it. Because if you know how all of the information that you're hearing in a discovery session fits together, you'll spend much less time thinking about where to put what you've heard – and you'll miss less. Session participants will be absolutely amazed by how you can capture so much information, and that you can so accurately describe their business processes.

Chapter 7. How to be an "Agile" Consultant

Contents

The keys to success for any consultant with this approach to business requirements analysis include many other best practices that have not been explored in this book. They are better left to other volumes, since this book is just about PowerStart Business Analysis. However, I do want to comment on a few things that will make your life as a consultant much better, and hopefully will help you be more "agile" in a real sense.

7.1 How to Source a 3rd Party Solution

Sourcing commercial off-the-shelf ("COTS") software can be a very painful and difficult exercise. It seems that most vendors have just one reply to questions about functionality and compatibility: *"Yes, our solution can do that!"*

As a consultant issuing an RFI, RFP or RFQ on behalf of your client to a vendor, your first objective should be to eliminate those vendors that can't support your client's business requirements. You already know that generalized statements outlining the business requirements won't accomplish this. In my experience, an effective way of clearing out the wannabees from the professionals is to give vendors a reasonably detailed statement of business requirements, which they can then assess against their own software product. This enables them to make specific reference to your requirements in addition to doing their usual selling job.

I have found the following approach to acquiring a COTS solution to be effective.

1. Identify a list of vendors who claim to have a software solution suitable to your client's business requirements (your 'long list', perhaps 6 to 10 vendors).

2. Conduct a ½-day or 1-day *Project Scope Blitz* to identify the *business events* the new COTS system must handle.

3. Prepare a <u>Request for Information</u> ('RFI') consisting of the following:

   (a) System Objectives (general introduction and overview).

   (b) Client Community Summary (who will use the system, which departments or groups, and where).

   (c) System Interfaces (required interfaces to your existing systems).

   (d) Hardware Interfaces (required interfaces to your existing technology and networks)

   (e) Software Interfaces (required compatibility with your existing software)

   (f) Communications Interfaces (required interfaces to your existing communications networks)

   (g) Other Interfaces (anything not mentioned above)

   (h) Audit, Control & Security Requirements (statements of required control and security levels)

   (i) Performance Criteria (minimum acceptable performance levels)

   (j) System Required Business Events (from the <u>Business Event list</u> developed in your *Project Scope Blitz* – this specifies required functionality)

Issue the RFI to the long list of vendors (6 to 10) and request their response by a specified deadline. Ask that their response specifically address each of the items listed – items (b) through (i) – and ask how their solution meets your specific environmental requirements.

Request that they also specifically address each of the *business events* on your list – item (j) – stating whether their solution handles each *business event* or not, but without details. Explain that short-listed vendors will have an opportunity to do detailed presentations.

Their responses should be written and emailed to you. Only short-listed vendors should be permitted to demonstrate their solution.

Ask them to include a cost overview (at a high level), including potential conversion costs for existing data, all hardware and software acquisition or lease costs, and the cost of training on the new system; as well as a potential installation schedule, conversion and full training of personnel, with a final 'up-and-running' target date. (This sounds like a lot of work for a vendor, but for the investment required by the buyer, it is a reasonable effort on their part.)

4. From the responses, shorten the list of vendors to two or three only. Notify those that have been successfully short-listed, and let them know about the next steps.

5. Ask each of the 2 or 3 short-listed vendors to demonstrate their system's functionality, based only on each *business event* stipulated in the original RFI.

6. After the event-specific demonstrations, recommend a vendor to your client, who can then negotiate terms, and acquire or lease the selected COTS solution.

These steps and the requirement for vendors to demonstrate their solutions based on individual *business events* help to keep them focused on the facts, and prevent the usual "dog and pony" show that's intended to solicit an emotional response to their proposal. This approach tells the vendors that you know exactly what you want, and that you have analyzed your requirements very carefully.

7.2 Keep a Master Business Events List

There are a limited number of *business events* in the world, and – yes – it is possible to collect your own list suitable to your organization and industry. My consulting firm has collected thousands of different and unique *business events* from all kinds of different projects. As a reader of this book, I'll be happy to send you a list of almost 4,000 *events*, organized by subject matter and industry. Just send me an email.

This kind of list helps consultants to conduct a comprehensive *Project Scope Blitz* with clients and – usually in less than a day – determine the size, ownership and duration of the requirements analysis for any project. By extracting project *business events* from a Master Business Events List, a consultant will be able to quickly preview them with clients, as part of the *Project Scope Blitz*, which will lead to a complete project-specific list even faster. Any organization, public or private, can accomplish this if the following is done:

• Collect and keep a Master Business Events List of all the *business events* you define for client organizations, as you apply these methods on different projects. Categorize the *business events* by business area and industry.

• For each new project, determine what *business events* on your Master Business Events List might be reusable on the new project. Do this as follows:

1. Make a copy of your Master Business Events List.

2. Remove all those *business events* that clearly do not apply.

3. Change the **nouns** in each *business event* statement to be the most likely nouns that will appear in the new project.

4. Select the *business events* that look like they will fit the new project.

Use this list of likely *business events* as input to your first step – the *Project Scope Blitz*. This gives you a good head start and saves a lot of time. As a consultant, it allows you to excel.

7.3 Debriefing Session Reviews

Usually, there's a post-project review – after the project is all said and done – to figure out what went well, what didn't and how to pass that information on for future projects.

The problem with this is that it's done – if it's done at all – after the project is done, which is way too late. Key issues will have been long forgotten by then, or not thought of as being as important as they were at the time they were encountered. I don't like post-project reviews any more than I like annual personnel reviews. It's simply way too late to be meaningful.

What to do instead?

After each discovery session, and after all information has been documented related to the process and data that supports a specific event – in other words, after about 4 hours of focused, event-specific work – hold a short debriefing session attended by the Pilot and co-pilot, and one other key person (perhaps one of your SMEs) who participated in building up that specific *business event*.

This should be a short session, usually not more than a half-hour. This debriefing session should cover three areas:

1. What worked well, so we can repeat it

2. What we learned that was new, so we can leverage it in future

3. What can be improved, so we can do a better job

Quickly document your findings, preferably in a Quality Management Wiki. Let your professional colleagues know about the new posting.

This debriefing process supports continual, immediate learning rather than an after-thought long into the project.

7.4 How to Get a Project Started

One of the biggest challenges for any consultant is the awkward issue of how to get a project started as quickly as possible. A consultant needs to be visible and productive just about right away because, well, clients think of them as people who can walk on water while so many others pass water. But, as we all know, consultants come in to an organization, have little background on what makes it tick or who has the knowledge, and are expected to become visibly productive just about right away. Well, here's a plan that has always worked for me.

The 5-Point Project Plan ...

A plan to uncover and specify business system requirements must be <u>specific</u> and <u>measurable</u>, not just another item on the list to be checked off. A plan must clearly identify what's to be done, by whom, and when. It must specify accurately the time and schedule involved. And it must be measurable – or it's just more of the **S**ame **O**ld **S**tuff made up of guesswork, magic numbers and unicorns.

1. **Initiate & Plan.** Working with your client, identify and document the following:

    *   The "co-pilot(s)" for the project. Whenever possible, you should have at least one. You, the consultant, are the Pilot.

    *   Project rationale, mandate, perceived scope, identified risks, expectations, and project budget.

    *   Stakeholders and subject-matter experts should be identified and their involvement clearly defined.

    *   The discovery session schedule. The initial entry will be the *Project Scope Blitz*, while the schedule for the detailed discovery sessions will be filled in later.

    *   The detailed list and definition of the deliverables and artifacts expected from the project business requirements analysis. This will be integrated into the overall Project Plan, which – if it entails staggered or phased delivery – must also include phased business analysis. This, too, is dependent on the outcome of the *Project Scope Blitz*.

    *   The metrics or KPI's[33] required to measure business analysis "success" for the project. Your success indicators will include, but are not limited to, a complete **Business Process Diagram** and all accompanying documentation for each *business event* identified; and documented business rules from each entry in the **Business Rules Table**.

---

[33] Key Performance Indicators.

- The acceptance and "sign off" process for the business requirements must be defined right up front.

Outcome: <u>Business Analysis Plan</u>.

2. **Conduct Project Scope Blitz.** Even if your client believes they have the scope all figured out, you will still conduct a *Project Scope Blitz*.

Stakeholders and SMEs must participate in a ½-day or 1-day *Project Scope Blitz*. This highly interactive session identifies clearly the conditions and circumstances the business must deal with (for your project), at a workable *business event* level, as well as the business areas and departments involved at each stage of business analysis. This enables you to schedule detailed discovery sessions. It also sets the tone for the project, right up front, and establishes your credibility as a servant leader and consultant.

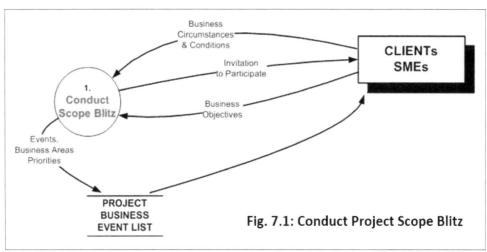

Fig. 7.1: Conduct Project Scope Blitz

Outcome: <u>Project Business Event List</u>.

3. **Plan Detailed Discovery Sessions.** Based on the *Project Business Event List*, create a schedule for each detailed discovery session and the SMEs required to participate. Also define the exact amount of time required to complete the project's business requirements analysis.

The resulting schedule is highly dynamic, based on your SMEs' availability and other priorities by the client.

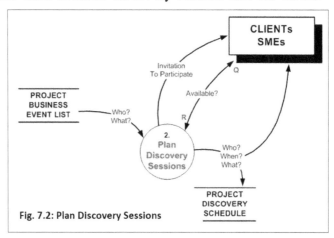

Fig. 7.2: Plan Discovery Sessions

However, deadlines can be set at this time. While the actual calendar dates of discovery sessions may change, the person-hours to complete should not.

   Outcome: <u>Project Discovery Schedule.</u>

4. **Conduct Detailed Discovery Sessions.** Based on the *Project Discovery Schedule*, invite the identified subject-matter experts and conduct interactive 1-hour discovery sessions for each *business event* to complete the business requirements for the project. Complete the remaining documentation for each *business event*.

   Outcome: <u>Business Requirements Document.</u>

5. **Coordinate Business Analysis Completion.** Depending on your mandate, you – as the consultant and "Pilot" for the project – will coordinate completion of the business analysis part of the project. The project may be phased or staged, which usually means you will "Pilot" each stage of business analysis. It will almost certainly extend into the solution design or software acquisition stage. If this is the case, it would be most productive if you were part of the team guiding the technology team through the business requirements.

   Lessons learned from all the discovery sessions are also integrated and documented now.

   Outcome: <u>Business Analysis Process Review.</u>

7.5 Apply Weinberg's 'Lump Law'

Partition the effort to minimize complexity. Break the project up into small, understandable and manageable pieces. Don't abstract. Develop one business process at a time. Partition groups of data into small, meaningful Objects. Focus on the individual questions from the **<u>Business Rules Table</u>**. Find one Object and ask one question at a time.

7.6 How to Fail without Really Trying Hard

There are lots of ways to really fail without too much effort. There are also lots of ways to win, which we have already discussed at length. Here's a short list of ways to get it dead wrong.

- Avoid the direct involvement of clients and subject-matter experts. (They really do have answers; we just have to ask them the right questions.)

- Guess at what the client might want. (Ask them, they really do have the answers.)

- Imagine that the client or SME doesn't know their business. (They do, you just have to ask them the questions right.)

- Worry about implementation issues too soon. (Figure out *what* before *how*.)

7.7 What Does an 'Agile' Environment Really Mean?

An "agile" project or agile environment is really a frame of mind, rather than a process. It's a paradigm or mental model of how we can approach our work. It's certainly not a methodology. An agile environment simply means, allow project teams to adapt working practices according to the needs of the individual project. The emphasis must be on delivering business value early, and then to continually improve it. "Delivering business value early" does not just refer to implementing software; it means to deliver value in how you interact with your business partners, clients and subject-matter experts ... and how you are seen to do so. It also means don't do anything you don't have to do and try to think outside the box to minimize doing things in a certain way just because they have always been done that way. But, to accomplish this you also have to recognize that (a) you are doing something that you may not need to do; and (b) what you're doing is only being done that way because it has always been done that way. In other words, you have to be aware of the conflict, which is easier said than done. If you're not an expert in the conventional approach, then how would you know if a different approach is better? What's your benchmark? What do you compare to?

'Agile' doesn't mean doing something differently just because you can do it differently. 'Agile' doesn't mean doing less of the project, just to beat the clock. 'Agile' means knowing which best practices really are "best" rather than conventional. There are lots of so-called best practices heralded by maintainers of the *status quo*. Bear in mind that "best practices" have usually been around a long time for them to be accepted as best practices by the community. Some of these "best practices" have passed their *best before* dates.

Also, 'agile' does not mean chaos on the project team. It means finding the straightest road to the planned destination, and then taking that road even when others think you should take the most circuitous and bureaucratic route possible.

'Agile' also means learning new methods and techniques, not blindly sticking with methods that haven't changed in years, and without any indication things are getting better. It also means to not avoid doing what's required (some of the administrative things) just because it seems faster that way. Times change; methods change.

The Agile Manifesto[34] stipulates the following as core values:

- **Individuals and interactions** over processes and tools. (I completely agree.)
- **Working software** over comprehensive documentation. (This doesn't need to be a trade-off. I believe you can have both, really fast.)
- **Customer collaboration** over contract negotiation. (I agree.)
- **Responding to change** over following a plan. (100% in agreement.)

Granted, some individuals and organizations have taken this too literally (which is always a danger when something is labeled a "manifesto"), which has led to challenged projects because of lack of professional discipline. There's more to a project than fast code. But when you read the Agile Manifesto completely you quickly discover that it is sound, well-reasoned, and embodies core principles that make good sense.

Above all, if you want to foster an agile environment, involve your clients and subject-matter experts in requirements discovery, and involve them a lot.

Your business requirements documentation should be in business language, and as brief as possible. And a client should not be expected to learn the technology you're using.

Recognize that you serve your client – whether that client is part of an internal group or a customer outside your organization – and you need their help and active participation to understand their requirements.

Recognize that requirements will change as your client understands better the information they want and can have. It's not a bad thing to "change your mind" when you have more information. As the famous British economist John Maynard Keynes once said, *"When the facts change, I change my opinion. What do you do?"*[35] The issue is how to deal with those changes, since history tells us that change is good. This is what learning is all about, so when a client or subject-matter expert changes their mind, don't think *"not on my project."* This is actually a move in the right direction.

I believe very strongly that requirements analysis should be focused on individual *business events*, and their supporting processes, rather than trying to write a novel about how a system should work.

By focusing on the individual *business event* and its supporting processes and data, you can respond very quickly to any change that is needed. It minimizes

---

[34] The complete Agile Alliance Manifesto can be found at www.AgileAlliance.org

[35] Quoted in **The Economist**, 24 October 1998, page 57.

the complexity of changing page after page in a serial novel. In event-based analysis, as I've described in this book, there is no redundancy; therefore, there is no domino effect[36] in the documentation. It allows the consultant/analyst to respond rapidly, while it gives the client or subject-matter expert the confidence to contribute without fear of criticism of "constantly changing their mind". Also, the direct 'BRT Questions' keep them highly focused, and they won't wander all over the scope of the requirements.

In my opinion, "agile" means being fast and responsive, but without chaos and risk.

An event-based approach to business requirements analysis is extremely fast, and without risk. The alternative – conventional system analysis that usually takes a long time – often leads to abbreviated requirements analysis (*"we finished when we ran out of time"*), which in turn leads to incomplete work down the line, and perhaps costly rework later on.

Some people refer to this event-based analysis approach as a "methodology". Well, so be it. I prefer to call it a paradigm – a constructive framework.[37] While Thomas Kuhn gave paradigm its contemporary meaning, I have tried to develop this event-based analysis paradigm on his definition:

- *what* is to be observed and scrutinized
- the kind of *questions* that are supposed to be asked and probed for answers in relation to this subject
- *how* these questions are to be structured
- *how* the results of scientific investigations should be interpreted

In the end, quality of work is always directly related to education, professional development training, experience, and the quality of the methods used and thinking applied.

Use good methods and clarity of thinking. Use modern methods. Practice using good methods and thinking. It gets better.

You will get very good at this by – yes, you guessed it – by practice. Just do it. Make mistakes. It's the only way we know of to become expert at anything.

Trond Frantzen
trond.frantzen@powerstartgroup.com

---

[36] A cumulative effect produced when one condition sets off a chain of similar events.

[37] Thomas Kuhn, in his controversial book *"The Structure of Scientific Revolutions"* used the term "paradigm shift". He also argued that rival paradigms are incommensurable – that is, it is not possible to understand one paradigm through the conceptual framework and terminology of another rival paradigm. I would certainly agree with that.

Appendix – List of Terms

Agile Environment: An "agile" business analysis environment simply means, try to think outside the box to <u>minimize doing things in a certain way just because they have always been done that way</u>. "Agile" does not mean chaos on the project team. It means finding the straightest road to your destination, and then taking that road even when others think you should take the most circuitous and bureaucratic route possible.

Anchor Object: An Object is an 'anchor' or 'cardinal' Object when it is used in the **Business Rules Table** to describe its relationship with other Objects and to define its business policies. It is the stable 'anchor' that is the subject of any question that is asked about its relationship with other participating Objects. This approach stipulates that every Object in a relationship is equally important (which certainly eliminates the high subjectivity of figuring out which one is *most important,* which is required by some methodologies) and therefore must be queried about its relationship with other Objects in a relationship. Since it takes two to make a relationship, each of the two Objects (from their own perspective) are the most important. Accordingly, every Object is the 'anchor' to a question. See also **'Object'**.

BRT	Salesperson	Customer
1 Salesperson		NA
1 Customer	1, N, 0	

These are the "anchor" Objects

Associative Object: An associative Object is an Object identified and created to remember essential information required in response to the occurrence of a *business event.* While it has all the attributes of any other kind of Object, it is also (a) dependent on some of the other Objects that participate in the same relationship; and (b) is created from the data that arises out of the process which supports the underlying relationship, since this new data cannot be found (by way of a *foreign key*) in any of the other Objects that participate in the same relationship. See also **'Object'**.

BRD: See **'Business Requirements Document'**.

BRT: See **'Business Rules Table'**.

Business Event: A *business event* is an essential business circumstance, condition, situation, state or external requirement that exists which the target business area must respond to or deal with in order to carry on operations to successfully support its key business objectives, goals, mission, direction and vision.

Business Interfaces Diagram: Also known as a 'Context Diagram' in some circles, this is a single process diagram representing a composite of all the *business events* and business

processes that make up the whole project or target system. The Business Interfaces Diagram illustrates what the target system communicates with other businesses, organizations, systems, or entities outside its own boundary. It is the highest, most abstract view of the system.

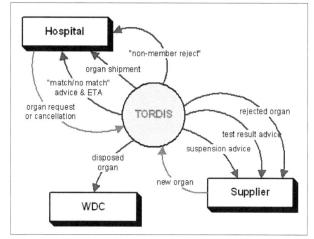

Business Process Diagram: This is an illustration of retrieval of data, the movement of data, and the recording of required data in a business process. A

single Business Process Diagram can support one or more *business events*. Each diagram must also have a narrative written in plain language to describe it. Objects that appear in a diagram must also be defined, with their data attributes, as well as the business rules that govern the behavior and existence of the Objects.

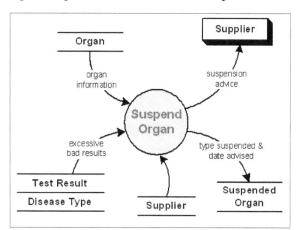

Business Requirements Document: The Business Requirements Document is all the documentation needed to represent all the business needs for a particular business area, project or system. It consists of diagrams showing all the required business processes, including descriptive narratives, Object definitions, data items that belong to Objects, and the business rules that govern the behavior and existence of the Objects. This document should be as free of technological bias as possible; i.e., it should document what is needed but not how it will be implemented.

Business Rule: These are the rules that govern the behavior and existence of Objects that support the business processes. Business rules are documented as simple declaratives under each Object (to which the rule is attributed) in plain language.

SUPPLIER

Business Rules
- We can receive one or more **PAYABLE ITEM**s from a **SUPPLIER**.
- We may never receive a **PAYABLE ITEM** from a **SUPPLIER** (e.g., may go out of business before we order a product; may not have been able to fill the only order from us).

Business Rules Table: This table is a unique tool that enables the discovery of the rules that govern the behavior and existence of Objects that support the business requirements. It ensures the completeness of the business requirements by using a specific syntax to determine the questions to be asked to uncover the rules (the 'BRT Questions'). It also identifies the 'ratio of occurrences' between Objects, therefore creating a prescription for eventual database design (a Conceptual Data Model) based on the business requirements.

	BRT	Salesperson	Customer	Outlet	Product	Payment
1	Salesperson		N,0	1,N	N,0	N,0
1	Customer	1,N,0		1,N	1,N,0	1,N,0
1	Outlet	N	N		N	N
1	Product	1,N,0	1,N,0	1,N		1,N,0
1	Payment	1,N	1	1	1,N	

Cardinality: This is the "ratio of occurrences" between pairs of Objects; i.e., 0, 1 and N, or any combination of these. See also **'Business Rules Table'.**

CASE Tool: An acronym for 'Computer Assisted Software Engineering' tool.

Characteristic Object: When two or more *related and inseparable* data items are discovered, each having multiple values for a single instance of an Object, this data group is separated from the original Object in which it was present, to form a new and distinct Object. For example, if a **SUPPLIER** Object has several locations, then data attributes like *supplier address* and *supplier city* will be part of a multi-valued (repeating) group. This multi-valued group of data items is separated from the originating or parent Object, and named **SUPPLIER LOCATION**, and is "characteristic" of the original Object.

Client: A client is one of the key stakeholders on a project. The client can also be one of the project's subject-matter experts.

<u>**Conceptual Data Model:**</u> The Conceptual Data Model is a prescription for access to information based on the needs of the business. It is a graphic that answers the question *"... can we get there from here?"* that's asked by database designers. This diagram is created by the database analysts and designers, based on the **Business Rules Table**. To complete the Conceptual Data Model, all Objects must be attributed with data and many-to-many relationships must be resolved.

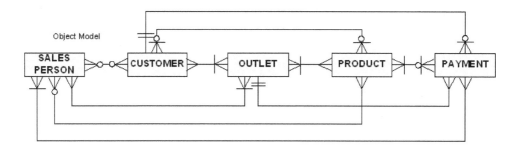

<u>**Context Diagram:**</u> See **'Business Interfaces Diagram'**.

<u>**Data Attribute:**</u> A data attribute is an element of data, which is a property of the Object to which it is attributed. A data attribute is described by a name and description, and eventually represented by a set of standard values, including sounds and images. Data attributes are required to define what must be remembered or known about each Object. See also **'Object'**.

PRODUCT

Data Attributes
- product description
- product photos & views (mv)
- examples of use (mv)
- product demonstrations (mv)
- product sounds (mv)
- reorder point
- product selling price
- volume discount available
- delivery lead time
- payment options (mv)
- product availability

<u>**Data Flow:**</u> A data flow represents the directional flow of information between a process and an Object or a Terminator.

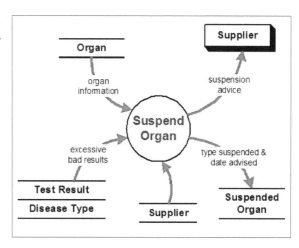

Denormalization: This is the process of adding controlled redundancies to a database design to improve efficiency. In a true relational model there can be no totals or status flags. A total is the sum of other fields or records, therefore it represents a duplication of data that already exists. A total violates Business Data Rule # 1 (*"Attribute the data item to the object it describes best, and to no other object"*). Denormalization – which is only done at database design time when all the facts about accesses, volumes and throughput rates are known – recognizes that it is sometimes better to build in 'controlled redundancy' such as a total to eliminate the need to read all those records. The same applies to a status flag. Status flags are often used to substitute for something else – which is clearly redundant – also violating Business Data Rule # 1. See also **'Normalization'**.

Discovery Session: See **'Requirements Discovery Session'**.

Exclusion Question (for Data): A question that identifies the consequences of excluding a data item by finding the *business event* the data item would otherwise support. See also **'Inclusion Question (for Data)'**.

Exclusion Question (for Objects): A question that identifies the consequences of excluding an Object by finding the *business event* the Object would otherwise support. See also **'Inclusion Question (for Objects)'**.

Exclusion Question (for Events): A question that identifies the consequences of excluding a *business event*. See also **'Inclusion Question (for Events)'**.

Exclusion Question (for Reports): A question that identifies the consequences of excluding a Report by finding the *business event* the Report would otherwise support. See also **'Inclusion Question (for Reports)'**.

Foreign Key: A foreign key is an Object's unique identifier contained within another Object. The foreign key provides the ability to find information from other related Objects to support the information needs of a specified business process. A foreign key is essentially an index or a pointer that 'joins' one Object to other related Objects. The 'joining' of Objects in this manner eliminates the need for redundant data repetition. A foreign key can be single-valued (i.e., point to one occurrence of another object); or it can be multi-valued (i.e., point to several instances of another Object). The ratio of occurrences (cardinality) between Objects is determined from the **Business Rules Table**.

CABLE ACCOUNT
Unique Identified
Cable Account-ID
Foreign Keys
Customer-ID (mv)
Rental-ID (mv)
Solution-ID (mv)
Promotion-ID (mv)

Inclusion Question (for Data): A question that identifies the necessity to include a data item by finding the *business event* the data items supports. See also **'Exclusion Question (for Data)'**.

Inclusion Question (for Objects): A question that identifies the necessity to include an Object by finding the *business event* the Object supports. See also **'Exclusion Question (for Objects)'**.

Inclusion Question (for Events): A question that identifies the necessity to include a *business event* by finding the consequences of including the *business event* (and therefore another *business event*). See also **'Exclusion Question (for Events)'**.

Inclusion Question (for Reports): A question that identifies the necessity to include a Report by finding the *business event* the Report supports. See also **'Exclusion Question (for Reports)'**.

JAD: (Joint Application Development) A JAD session is very similar to a requirements discovery session, as described in this book. JAD was developed by Chuck Morris of IBM Raleigh and Tony Crawford of IBM Toronto in the late 1970s. In 1980 Crawford and Morris taught JAD in Toronto and Crawford led several workshops to prove the concept. The results were good and JAD became a well-accepted best practice in many companies. In time, JAD developed and gained general approval in the corporate world. Crawford defines JAD as an interactive systems design concept involving discussion groups in a workshop setting. Originally, JAD was designed to bring system developers and users of varying backgrounds and opinions together in a productive and creative environment. The meetings were a way of obtaining quality requirements and specifications. This provided a good alternative to previously traditional serial interviews by system analysts. See also **'Requirements Discovery Session'**.

Multi-valued (Repeating) Group: See **'Characteristic Object'**.

Normalization: "Normalization" is a commonly accepted method of eliminating data redundancies. The science underlying normalization theory is quite complex and normally requires considerable study. However, only researchers and teachers need this degree of familiarity with normalization theory and all its abstractions. Business analysts need to know how to do it so good Objects can be defined to support business processes – 'good' meaning Objects that are focused, and not a mixed bag of all kinds of data about all kinds of stuff. Knowing the details of the theory does not enhance our ability to deliver a business requirement with "fully normalized" data to support it. Scores of books have been written about this subject, so you can learn as much about the underlying theory as you want by searching on the Internet or buying a few good technical books. But to get a "normalized" data set for your project simply means following the **5 Rules of Business Data**. These Rules, when followed, will deliver a view of the data that is sufficiently "normalized" with redundancies minimized.

It should be noted that the conventional view is that normalization is "done" after all the needed data has been gathered and attributed to Objects, in a step-wise progression through different levels of normalization. While this does work, it also takes a very long time to do, and is very frustrating to people who want to get on with the work. The conventional approach is not an agile approach.

Using the methods in the book, normalization is done immediately when specific data is discovered. The data attribution rules are applied <u>during the process of data discovery</u>, not afterwards. Accordingly, it's done right away as a natural and inherent part of business system analysis. See also **'Denormalization'.**

<u>Object (in an Object-Relationship Diagram):</u> An Object (sometimes called an *entity*) is a person, place or thing that the target business area needs to know or remember something about. An Object is a noun, but it is distinct from other nouns that are data attributes because a <u>business</u> Object (1) consists of two or more data attributes to give it 'substance'; (2) is <u>essential</u> to the successful operation of the target business area to meet client objectives (i.e., the Object *must* be present); and (3) is defined by its business rules and data attributes. All <u>business</u> Objects must consist of two or more data attributes, but these objects can be 'normalized' to just a single data attribute when finalizing the physical database design.

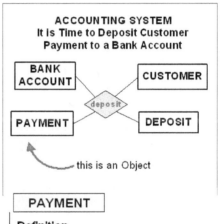

this is an Object

PAYMENT

Definition

A financial instrument offered by a customer in exchange for the company's products.

Business Rules

- Is credited to one sales person only (i.e., there are no split commissions)
- Is from one customer only
- Can only be received in one outlet
- Must be for one or many products (i.e., future payments and credits are not accepted)
- Must be for one or more sales transactions (i.e., payments against future transactions are not accepted)

Data Attributes

- payment date
- method of payment
- amount of payment
- type of card
- card expiry date

Object (in a Business Process Diagram): Objects that appear in Business Process Diagrams are the exact same Objects as defined in an Object-Relationship Diagram. Objects that are present in a process diagram were often called "data stores" in their earlier incarnation. See also **'Business Process Diagram'**.

Object-Relationship Diagram: This is a picture of the information that we need to know about (retrieve) or remember (record), in a specific context. It shows how groups of related information (Objects) are joined together, and the circumstance (i.e., the *business event*) under which they are associated with other groups of data (Objects). This type of diagram can be one of the components of the business requirements, if the new system is research-based or data warehouse oriented rather than process-based. These diagrams do not show the flow of data in a process, except for the verb in the diamond (the relationship) that joins the Objects together.

Process Narrative: A Business Process Diagram must always have a narrative written in plain language to describe it. The narrative can be written in several styles, the most common being 'Point Form Style' and the 'Structured Narrative Style'.

Point Form Style

For each request for a product from the customer:

- Find out if the customer exists in our system.
- Find the product sold.
- If it is available, give it to the customer with the price.
- Accept the payment from the customer.
- Remember the payment.
- Remember the salesperson who served the customer, and in which outlet.
- Reduce inventory by the quantity of product sold.
- If it is a new customer, get the customer information from the customer.
- Remember the new customer information.

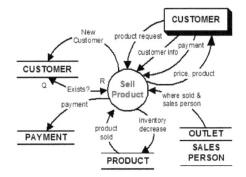

Structured Narrative Style

For each request for a product from the customer, find the product. If it is available give it to the customer with the cost. Accept the payment from the customer. Remember the payment and the sales transaction, including the sales person who served the customer, and in which outlet. Reduce inventory by the quantity of the product sold. If it is a new customer, remember the customer.

Ratio of Occurrences: See **'Cardinality'**.

Requirements Discovery Session: An interactive meeting of project clients and subject-matter experts, led by an expert "Pilot" and possibly supported by an expert "co-pilot", with the purpose of discovering business requirements. See also **'JAD'**.

SME: See also **'Subject-Matter Expert'**.

Subject-Matter Expert: An individual who may or may not be the client. Subject-matter experts are individuals who have all the required knowledge about the business areas and information that's involved in the targeted processes. A subject-matter expert should never be a surrogate client who does not work hands-on in the business area for which they are expert.

Subtype Object: A "subtype Object" (a.k.a. 'subclass') is a type of Object which has only those data attributes that are specific to a particular view of the Object (i.e., the subtype). Data attributed to one subtype Object cannot be attributed to any other Object. Data which is common to more than one subtype is attributed to the Object associated with the subtype, which is called a supertype Object. Each subtype Object must be associated with only one supertype Object. See also **'Supertype Object'** and **'Object'**.

Supertype Object: A "supertype Object" (a.k.a. 'superclass') is an Object that has several different views of the information it represents, with each distinct view known as a subtype Object. Each subtype of a supertype Object has unique and distinct data attributes. Supertype Objects contain only the data attributes that are common to all its subtypes. See also **'Subtype Object'** and **'Object'**.

Terminator: A Terminator is an external entity over which the business process it communicates with has no control. The Terminator can be outside the organization, or inside, but it is always external to the process that communicates with it. It acts as a source of input information, or a destination of information from the business process, but the processes and data inside a terminator are outside the scope of the target system. Many (but not all) terminators are also Objects, since we usually have to remember something about them.

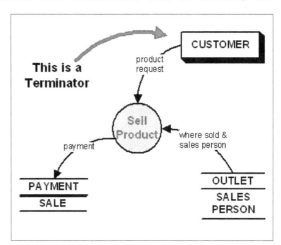

Unique Identifier: A primary identifier or *key* is a unique identifier of a specific instance of an Object. The unique identifier should never contain data to be used in a process. It is simply a locator address. See also **'Object'**.

How to Get from Here to There